MORE
THAN A
CARPENTER

MORE
THAN A
CARPENTER

JOSH McDOWELL

Tyndale House Publishers, Inc.
Wheaton, Illinois

Scripture quotations in this book are taken from the New
American Standard Bible, unless otherwise indicated.

Library of Congress Catalog Card Number 76-58135. ISBN
0-8423-4550-7, paper. Copyright © 1977 by Tyndale House
Publishers, Inc., Wheaton, Illinois. All rights reserved. First
printing, April 1977. Printed in the United States of America.

CONTENTS

To Dick and Charlotte Day
whose lives have always
reflected that Jesus was
more than a carpenter.

Preface

Almost 2,000 years ago, Jesus entered the human race in a small Jewish community. He was a member of a poor family, a minority group, and resided in one of the smallest countries in the world. He lived approximately thirty-three years, of which only the last three comprised his public ministry.

Yet people almost everywhere still remember him. The date of our morning newspaper or the copyright date of a university textbook bears witness to the fact that Jesus lived one of the greatest lives ever lived.

H. G. Wells, the noted historian, was asked which person had left the most permanent impression on history. He replied that if one judged a person's greatness by historical standards, "By this test Jesus stands first."

PREFACE

Historian Kenneth Scott Latourette said: "As the centuries pass, the evidence is accumulating that, measured by his effect on history, Jesus is the most influential life ever lived on this planet. That influence appears to be mounting."

From Ernest Renan we have the following observation: "Jesus was the greatest religious genius that ever lived. His beauty is eternal, and his reign shall never end. Jesus is in every respect unique, and nothing can be compared with him. All history is incomprehensible without Christ."

1
What Makes Jesus So Different?

Recently I was talking with a group of people in Los Angeles. I asked them, "Who, in your opinion, is Jesus Christ?" The response was that he was a great religious leader. I agree with that. Jesus Christ was a great religious leader. But I believe he was much more.

Men and women down through the ages have been divided over the question, "Who is Jesus?" Why so much conflict over one individual? Why is it that his name, more than the name of any other religious leader, causes irritation? Why is it that you can talk about God and nobody gets upset, but as soon as you mention Jesus, people so often want to stop the conversation? Or they become defensive. I mentioned something about Jesus to a taxicab driver in London, and immediately he said, "I don't like to discuss religion, especially Jesus."

How is Jesus different from other religious leaders? Why don't the names of Buddha, Mohammed, Confucius offend people? The reason is that these others didn't claim to be God, but Jesus did. That is what makes him so different from other religious leaders.

It didn't take long for the people who knew Jesus to realize that he was making astounding claims about himself. It became clear that his own claims were identifying him as more than just a prophet or teacher. He was obviously making claims to deity. He was presenting himself as the only avenue to a relationship with God, the only source of forgiveness for sins, and the only way of salvation.

For many people this is too exclusive, too narrow for them to want to believe. Yet the issue is not what do we want to think or believe, but rather, who did Jesus claim to be?

What do the New Testament documents tell us about this? We often hear the phrase, "the deity of Christ." This means that Jesus Christ is God.

A. H. Strong in his *Systematic Theology* defines God as the "infinite and perfect spirit in whom all things have their source, support, and end."[1] This definition of God is adequate for all theists, including Muslims and Jews. Theism teaches that God is personal and that the universe was planned and created by him. God sustains and rules it in the present. Christian theism adds an additional note to the above definition: "and who became incarnate as Jesus of Nazareth."

Jesus Christ is actually a name and a title. The name Jesus is derived from the Greek form of the name *Jeshua* or Joshua meaning "Jehovah-Savior" or "the Lord saves." The title Christ is derived from the Greek word for Messiah (or the Hebrew *Mashiach*—Daniel 9:26) and means "anointed one." Two offices, king and priest, are involved in the use of the title "Christ." His title affirms Jesus as the promised priest and king of Old Testament prophecies. This affirmation is one of the crucial areas for having a proper understanding about Jesus and Christianity.

The New Testament clearly presents Christ as God. The names applied to Christ in the New Testament are such that they could properly be applied only to one who was God. For example, Jesus is called God in the phrase, "Looking for the blessed hope and the appearing of the glory of our great God and Savior, Christ Jesus" (Titus 2:13; compare John 1:1; Hebrews 1:8; Romans 9:5; 1 John 5:20, 21). The Scriptures attribute characteristics to him that can be true only of God. Jesus is presented as being self-existent (John 1:4; 14:6); omnipresent (Matthew 28:20; 18:20); omniscient (John 4:16; 6:64; Matthew 17:22–27); omnipotent (Revelation 1:8; Luke 4:39–55; 7:14, 15; Matthew 8:26, 27); and possessing eternal life (1 John 5:11, 12, 20; John 1:4).

11

Jesus received honor and worship that only God should receive. In a confrontation with Satan, Jesus said, "It is written, 'You shall worship the Lord your God, and serve Him only'" (Matthew 4:10). Yet Jesus received worship as God (Matthew 14:33; 28:9) and sometimes even demanded to be worshiped as God (John 5:23; compare Hebrews 1:6; Revelation 5:8–14).

Most of the followers of Jesus were devout Jews who believed in one true God. They were monotheistic to the core, yet they recognized him as God incarnate.

Because of his extensive rabbinical training, Paul would be even less likely to attribute deity to Jesus, to worship a man from Nazareth and call him Lord. But this is exactly what Paul did. He acknowledged the Lamb of God (Jesus) as God when he said, "Be on guard for yourselves and for all the flock, among which the Holy Spirit has made you overseers, to shepherd the church of God which He purchased with His own blood" (Acts 20:28).

Peter confessed, after Christ asked him who he was: "Thou art the Christ, the Son of the living God" (Matthew 16:16). Jesus responded to Peter's confession not by correcting his conclusion but by acknowledging its validity and source: "Blessed are you, Simon Barjona, because flesh and blood did not reveal this to you, but My Father who is in heaven" (Matthew 16:17).

Martha, a close friend of Jesus, said to him, "I

have believed that You are the Christ [Messiah], the Son of God" (John 11:27). Then there is Nathanael, who didn't think anything good could come out of Nazareth. He acknowledged that Jesus was "the Son of God; You are the King of Israel" (John 1:49).

While Stephen was being stoned, "he called upon the Lord and said, 'Lord Jesus, receive my spirit!'" (Acts 7:59). The writer of Hebrews calls Christ God when he writes, "But of the Son He says, 'Thy throne, O God, is forever and ever'" (Hebrews 1:8). John the Baptist announced the coming of Jesus by saying that "the Holy Spirit descended upon Him in bodily form like a dove, and a voice came out of heaven, 'Thou art My beloved Son, in Thee I am well-pleased" (Luke 3:22).

Then of course we have the confession of Thomas, better known as the "The Doubter." Perhaps he was a graduate student. He said, "I won't believe unless I can put my finger into his nail scars." I identify with Thomas. He said, "Look, not every day does someone raise himself from the dead or claim to be God incarnate. I need evidence." Eight days later, after Thomas chronicled his doubts about Jesus before the other disciples, "Jesus came, the doors having been shut, and stood in their midst, and said, 'Peace be with you.' Then He said to Thomas, 'Reach here your finger, and see My hands; and reach here your hand, and put it into My side; and be not unbelieving, but believing.' Thomas answered and said to Him, 'My Lord and my God!' Jesus said to him, 'Because you have seen Me, have you believed? Blessed are they who did not see, and yet believed'" (John 20:26–29). Jesus accepted Thomas's acknowledgment of him as God. He rebuked Thomas for his unbelief, but not for his worship.

At this point a critic may interject that all these references are from others about Christ, not from Christ about himself. The accusation in the classroom is usually that those at the time of Christ misunderstood him as we are misunderstanding him today. In other words, Jesus really didn't claim to be God.

Well, I think he did, and I believe that the deity of Christ is derived directly from the pages of the New Testament. The references are abundant and their meaning is plain. A businessman who scrutinized the Scriptures to verify whether or not Christ claimed to be God said, "For anyone to read the New Testament and not conclude that Jesus claimed to be divine, he would have to be as blind as a man standing outdoors on a clear day and saying he can't see the sun."

In the Gospel of John we have a confrontation between Jesus and some Jews. It was triggered by Jesus' curing a lame man on the Sabbath and telling him to pick up his pallet and walk. "And for this reason the Jews were persecuting Jesus, because He was doing these things on the Sabbath. But He answered them, 'My Father is working until now, and I Myself am working.' For this cause therefore the Jews were seeking all the more to kill Him, because He not only was breaking the Sabbath, but also was calling God His own Father, making Himself equal with God" (John 5:16–18).

You might say, "Look, Josh, I can say, 'My father is working until now, and I myself am working.' So what? It doesn't prove anything." Whenever we study a document, we must take into account the language, the culture, and especially the person or persons addressed. In this case, the culture is Jewish and the persons addressed are Jewish religious leaders. Let's see how the Jews understood Jesus' remarks 2,000 years ago in their own culture. "For this cause therefore the Jews were seeking all the more to kill Him, because He not only was breaking the Sabbath, but also was calling God His own Father, making Himself equal with God" (John 5:18). Why such a drastic reaction?

The reason is that Jesus said "*my* Father," not "our Father," and then added "is working until now." Jesus' use of these two phrases made himself equal with God, on a par with God's activity. The Jews did not refer to God as "my Father." Or if they did, they would qualify the statement with "in heaven." However, Jesus did not do this. He made a claim that the Jews could not misinterpret when he called God "my Father." Jesus also implied that while God was working, he, the Son, was working too. Again, the Jews understood the implication that he was God's Son. As a result of this statement, the Jews' hatred grew. Even though they were seeking, mainly, to persecute him, they then began to desire to kill him.

Not only did Jesus claim equality with God as his Father, but he also asserted that he was one with the Father. During the Feast of the Dedication in Jerusalem, Jesus was approached by some Jewish leaders who asked about his being the Christ. Jesus ended his comments to them by saying, "I and the Father are one" (John 10:30). "The Jews took up stones again to stone Him. Jesus answered them, 'I showed you many good works from the Father; for which of them are you stoning Me?' The Jews answered Him, 'For a good work we do not stone You, but for blasphemy; and because You, being a man, make Yourself out to be God'" (John 10:31–33).

One might wonder why there was such a strong reaction to what Jesus said about being one with the Father. An interesting implication of this phrase arises when the Greek is studied. Greek scholar A. T. Robertson writes that the "one" is neuter, not masculine, in the Greek, and does not indicate one in person or purpose but rather one in "essence or nature." Robertson then adds: "This crisp statement is the climax of Christ's claims about the relation between the Father and himself [the Son]. They stir the Pharisees to uncontrollable anger."[2]

It is evident then that in the minds of those who

16

heard this statement there was no doubt that Jesus claimed he was God. Thus, Leon Morris, principal of Ridley College, Melbourne, writes that "the Jews could regard Jesus' word only as blasphemy, and they proceeded to take the judgment into their own hands. It was laid down in the Law that blasphemy was to be punished by stoning (Lev. 24:16). But these men were not allowing the due processes of law to take their course. They were not preparing an indictment so that the authorities could take the requisite action. In their fury they were preparing to be judges and executioners in one."[3]

Jesus is threatened with stoning for "blasphemy." The Jews definitely understood his teaching but, we may ask, did they stop to consider whether his claims were true or not?

Jesus continuously spoke of himself as one in essence and nature with God. He boldly asserted, "If you knew Me, you would know My Father also" (John 8:19); "He who beholds me beholds the One who sent me" (John 12:45); "He who hates Me, hates My Father also" (John 15:23); "All may honor the Son, even as they honor the Father. He who does not honor the Son does not honor the Father who sent Him" (John 5:23); etc. These references certainly indicate that Jesus looked at himself as being more than just a man; rather, he was equal with God. Those who say that Jesus was just closer or more intimate with God than others need to think about his statement, "If you do not honor me as you honor the Father, you dishonor us both."

When I was lecturing in a literature class at the University of West Virginia, a professor interrupted me and said that the only Gospel in which Jesus claimed to be God was John's Gospel and it was the latest one written. He then asserted that Mark, the earliest Gospel, never once mentioned Jesus' claiming to be God. It was obvious this man hadn't read Mark—or hadn't paid much attention to what he read.

In response I turned to Mark's Gospel. There Jesus claimed to be able to forgive sins. "And Jesus seeing their faith said to the paralytic, 'My son, your sins are forgiven'" (Mark 2:5; see also Luke 7:48–50). By Jewish law this was something only God could do; Isaiah 43:25 restricts this prerogative to God alone. The scribes asked, "Why does this man speak that way? He is blaspheming; who can forgive sins but God alone?" (Mark 2:7). Jesus then asked which would be easier, to say "Your sins are forgiven"; or to say "Arise and walk"?

According to the Wycliffe Commentary, this is "an unanswerable question. The statements are equally simple to pronounce; but to say either, with accompanying performance, requires divine power. An imposter, of course, in seeking to avoid detection, would find the former easier. Jesus proceeded to heal the illness that men might know that he had authority to deal with its cause."[4] At this he was accused of blasphemy by the religious leaders. Lewis Sperry Chafer writes that "none on earth has either authority or right to forgive sin. None could forgive sin save the One against whom all have sinned. When Christ forgave sin, as He certainly did, He was not exercising a human prerogative. Since none but God can forgive sins, it is conclusively demonstrated that Christ, since He forgave sins, is God."[5]

This concept of forgiveness bothered me for quite awhile because I didn't understand it. One day in a philosophy class, answering a question about the deity of Christ, I quoted the above verses from Mark. A graduate assistant challenged my conclusion that Christ's forgiveness demonstrated his deity. He said that he could forgive someone and that wouldn't demonstrate he was claiming to be God. As I pondered what the graduate assistant was saying, it struck me why the religious leaders reacted against Christ. Yes, one can say, "I forgive you," but that can be done only by the person who was sinned against. In other words, if you sin against me, I can say, "I forgive you." But that wasn't what Christ was doing. The paralytic had sinned against God the Father and then Jesus, under his own authority, said, "Your sins are forgiven." Yes, we can forgive injuries committed against us, but in no way can anyone forgive sins committed against God except God himself. That is what Jesus did.

No wonder the Jews reacted when a carpenter

from Nazareth made such a bold claim. This power of Jesus to forgive sin is a startling example of his exercising a prerogative that belongs to God alone.

Also in the Gospel of Mark we have the trial of Jesus (14:60–64). Those trial proceedings are one of the clearest references to Jesus' claims of deity. "And the high priest arose and came forward and questioned Jesus, saying, 'Do You make no answer to what these men are testifying against You?' But He kept silent, and made no answer. Again the high priest was questioning Him, and saying to Him, 'Are You the Christ, the Son of the Blessed One?' And Jesus said, 'I am; and you shall see the Son of Man sitting at the right hand of Power, and coming with the clouds of heaven.' And tearing his clothes, the high priest said, 'What further need do we have of witnesses? You have heard the blasphemy; how does it seem to you?' And they all condemned Him to be deserving of death."

At first Jesus wouldn't answer, so the high priest put him under oath. Being under oath Jesus had to answer (and I'm so glad he did). He responded to the question, "Are You the Christ, the son of the Blessed One?" by saying "I am."

An analysis of Christ's testimony shows that he claimed to be (1) the Son of the Blessed One (God); (2) the One who would sit at the right hand of power, and (3) the Son of Man who would come on the clouds of heaven. Each of the affirmations is distinctively messianic. The cumulative effect of all three is significant. The Sanhedrin, the Jewish court, caught all three points, and the high priest responded by tearing his garments and saying, "What further need do we have of witnesses?" They had finally heard it from him themselves. He was convicted by the words of his own mouth.

Robert Anderson points out: "No confirmatory evidence is more convincing than that of hostile witnesses, and the fact that the Lord laid claim to Deity is incontestably established by the action of His enemies. We must remember that the Jews were not a tribe of ignorant savages, but a highly cultured and intensely religious people; and it was upon this very charge that, without a dissenting voice, His death was decreed by the Sanhedrin—their great national Council, composed of the most eminent of their religious leaders, including men of the type of Gamaliel and his great pupil, Saul of Tarsus."[6]

It is clear, then, that this is the testimony Jesus wanted to bear about himself. We also see that the Jews understood his reply as a claim to his being God. There were two alternatives to be faced then; that his assertions were blasphemy, or that he was God. His judges saw the issue clearly—so clearly, in fact, that they crucified him and then taunted him because "He trusted in God . . . for He said, 'I am the Son of God' " (Matthew 27:43).

H. B. Swete explains the significance of the high

21

priest tearing his garment: "The law forbade the
High Priest to rend his garment in private troubles
(Leviticus 10:6; 21:10), but when acting as a judge,
he was required by custom to express in this way
his horror of any blasphemy uttered in his presence. The relief of the embarrassed judge is mani-
fest. If trustworthy evidence was not forthcoming,
the necessity for it had now been superseded: the
Prisoner had incriminated Himself."[7]

We begin to see that this was no ordinary trial,
as lawyer Irwin Linton brings out: "Unique among
criminal trials is this one in which not the actions
but the identity of the accused is the issue. The
criminal charge laid against Christ, the confession
or testimony or, rather, act in presence of the
court, on which He was convicted, the interroga-
tion by the Roman governor and the inscription
and proclamation on His cross at the time of
execution all are concerned with the one question
of Christ's real identity and dignity. 'What think
ye of Christ? Whose son is he?' "[8]

Judge Gaynor, the accomplished jurist of the
New York bench, in his address on the trial of
Jesus, takes the position that blasphemy was the
one charge made against him before the Sanhedrin. He says: "It is plain from each of the gospel
narratives, that the alleged crime for which Jesus
was tried and convicted was blasphemy: . . .
Jesus had been claiming supernatural power,
which in a human being was blasphemy"[9] (citing
John 10:33). (Gaynor's reference is to Jesus' "mak-

22

ing himself God," not to what he said about the Temple.)

In most trials, people are tried for what they have done, but this was not true of Christ's. Jesus was tried for who he was.

The trial of Jesus ought to be sufficient to demonstrate convincingly that he confessed his divinity. His judges witness to that. But also, on the day of his crucifixion, his enemies acknowledged that he claimed to be God come in the flesh. "In the same way the chief priests, along with the scribes and elders, were mocking Him, and saying, 'He saved others; He cannot save Himself. He is the King of Israel; let Him now come down from the cross, and we shall believe in Him. He trusts in God; let Him deliver Him now, if He takes pleasure in Him; for He said, "I am the son of God"'" (Matthew 27:41–43).

NOTES ON CHAPTER 1

1. A. H. Strong, *Systematic Theology*. (Philadelphia: Judson Press, 1907), Vol. 1, p. 52.
2. Archibald Thomas Robertson, *Word Pictures in the New Testament* (Nashville: Broadman Press, 1932), Vol. 5, p. 186.
3. Leon Morris, "The Gospel According to John," *The New International Commentary on The New Testament* (Grand Rapids: William B. Eerdmans Publishing Co., 1971), p. 524.
4. Charles F. Pfeiffer, and Everett F. Harrison (Eds.), *The Wycliffe Bible Commentary* (Chicago: Moody Press, 1962), pp. 943, 944.

5. Lewis Sperry Chafer, *Systematic Theology* (Dallas Theological Seminary Press, 1947, Vol. 5), p. 21.
6. Robert Anderson, *The Lord from Heaven* (London: James Nisbet and Co., Ltd., 1910), p. 5.
7. Henry Barclay Swete, *The Gospel According to St. Mark* (London: Macmillan and Co., Ltd., 1898), p. 339.
8. Irwin H. Linton, *The Sanhedrin Verdict* (New York: Loizeaux Brothers, Bible Truth Depot, 1943), p. 7.
9. Charles Edmund Deland, *The Mis-Trials of Jesus* (Boston: Richard G. Badger, 1914), pp. 118–119.

2

Lord, Liar,
or Lunatic?

The distinct claims of Jesus to be God eliminate the popular ploy of skeptics who regard Jesus as just a good moral man or a prophet who said a lot of profound things. So often that conclusion is passed off as the only one acceptable to scholars or as the obvious result of the intellectual process. The trouble is, many people nod their heads in agreement and never see the fallacy of such reasoning.

To Jesus, who men and women believed him to be was of fundamental importance. To say what Jesus said and to claim what he claimed about himself, one couldn't conclude he was just a good moral man or prophet. That alternative isn't open to an individual, and Jesus never intended it to be.

C. S. Lewis, who was a professor at Cambridge

University and once an agnostic, understood this issue clearly. He writes: "I am trying here to prevent anyone saying the really foolish thing that people often say about Him: 'I'm ready to accept Jesus as a great moral teacher, but I don't accept His claim to be God.' That is the one thing we must not say. A man who was merely a man and said the sort of things Jesus said would not be a great moral teacher. He would either be a lunatic—on a level with the man who says he is a poached egg—or else he would be the Devil of Hell. You must make your choice. Either this man was, and is, the Son of God: or else a madman or something worse."

Then Lewis adds: "You can shut Him up for a fool, you can spit at Him and kill Him as a demon; or you can fall at His feet and call Him Lord and God. But let us not come up with any patronising nonsense about His being a great human teacher. He has not left that open to us. He did not intend to."[1]

F. J. A. Hort, who spent twenty-eight years in a critical study of the New Testament text, writes: "His words were so completely parts and utterances of Himself, that they had no meaning as abstract statements of truth uttered by Him as a Divine oracle or prophet. Take away Himself as the primary (though not the ultimate) subject of every statement and they all fall to pieces."[2]

In the words of Kenneth Scott Latourette, historian of Christianity at Yale University: "It is not his teachings which make Jesus so remarkable, although these would be enough to give him distinction. It is a combination of the teachings with the man himself. The two cannot be separated." "It must be obvious," Latourette concludes, "to any thoughtful reader of the Gospel records that Jesus regarded himself and his message as inseparable. He was a great teacher, but he was more. His teachings about the kingdom of God, about human conduct, and about God were important, but they could not be divorced from him without, from his standpoint, being vitiated."[3]

Jesus claimed to be God. He didn't leave any other option open. His claim must be either true or false, so it is something that should be given serious consideration. Jesus' question to his disciples, "But who do you say that I am?" (Matthew 16:15) has several alternatives.

First, consider that his claim to be God was false. If it was false, then we have two and only two alternatives. He either knew it was false or he didn't know it was false. We will consider each one separately and examine the evidence.

WAS HE A LIAR?

If, when Jesus made his claims, he knew that he was not God, then he was lying and deliberately deceiving his followers. But if he was a liar, then he was also a hypocrite because he told others to

27

be honest, whatever the cost, while he himself taught and lived a colossal lie. More than that, he was a demon, because he told others to trust him for their eternal destiny. If he couldn't back up his claims and knew it, then he was unspeakably evil. Last, he would also be a fool because it was his claims to being God that led to his crucifixion.

Many will say that Jesus was a good moral teacher. Let's be realistic. How could he be a great moral teacher and knowingly mislead people at the most important point of his teaching—his own identity?

You would have to conclude logically that he was a deliberate liar. This view of Jesus, however, doesn't coincide with what we know either of him or the results of his life and teachings. Wherever Jesus has been proclaimed, lives have been changed for the good, nations have changed for the better, thieves are made honest, alcoholics are cured, hateful individuals become channels of love, unjust persons become just.

William Lecky, one of Great Britain's most noted historians and a dedicated opponent of organized Christianity, writes: "It was reserved for Christianity to present to the world an ideal character which through all the changes of eighteen centuries has inspired the hearts of men with an impassioned love; has shown itself capable of acting on all ages, nations, temperaments and conditions; has been not only the highest pattern of virtue, but the strongest incentive to its practice. . . . The simple record of these three short years of active life has done more to regenerate and soften mankind than all the disquisitions of philosophers and all the exhortations of moralists."[4]

Historian Philip Schaff says: "This testimony, if not true, must be downright blasphemy or madness. The former hypothesis cannot stand a moment before the moral purity and dignity of Jesus, revealed in his every word and work, and acknowledged by universal consent. Self-deception in a matter so momentous, and with an intellect in all respects so clear and so sound, is equally out of the question. How could he be an enthusiast or a madman who never lost the even balance of his mind, who sailed serenely over all the troubles and persecutions, as the sun above the clouds, who always returned the wisest answer to tempting questions, who calmly and deliberately predicted his death on the cross, his resurrection on the third day, the outpouring of the Holy Spirit, the founding of his Church, the destruction of Jerusalem—predictions which have been literally fulfilled? A character so original, so complete, so uniformly consistent, so perfect, so human and yet so high above all human greatness, can be neither a fraud nor a fiction. The poet, as has been well said, would in this case be greater than the hero. It would take more than a Jesus to invent a Jesus."[5]

Elsewhere Schaff gives convincing argument

against Christ being a liar: "How, in the name of logic, common sense, and experience, could an impostor—that is a deceitful, selfish, depraved man—have invented, and consistently maintained from the beginning to end, the purest and noblest character known in history with the most perfect air of truth and reality? How could he have conceived and successfully carried out a plan of unparalleled beneficence, moral magnitude, and sublimity, and sacrificed his own life for it, in the face of the strongest prejudices of his people and age?"[6]

If Jesus wanted to get people to follow him and believe in him as God, why did he go to the Jewish nation? Why go as a Nazarene carpenter to a country so small in size and population and so thoroughly adhering to the undivided unity of God? Why didn't he go to Egypt or, even more, to Greece, where they believed in various gods and various manifestations of them?

Someone who lived as Jesus lived, taught as Jesus taught, and died as Jesus died could not have been a liar. What other alternatives are there?

WAS HE A LUNATIC?

If it is inconceivable for Jesus to be a liar, then couldn't he actually have thought himself to be God, but been mistaken? After all, it's possible to

30

be both sincere and wrong. But we must remember that for someone to think himself God, especially in a fiercely monotheistic culture, and then to tell others that their eternal destiny depended on believing in him, is no slight flight of fantasy but the thoughts of a lunatic in the fullest sense. Was Jesus Christ such a person?

Someone who believes he is God sounds like someone today believing himself Napoleon. He would be deluded and self-deceived, and probably he would be locked up so he wouldn't hurt himself or anyone else. Yet in Jesus we don't observe the abnormalities and imbalance that usually go along with being deranged. His poise and composure would certainly be amazing if he were insane.

Noyes and Kolb, in a medical text,[7] describe the schizophrenic as a person who is more autistic than realistic. The schizophrenic desires to escape from the world of reality. Let's face it; claiming to be God would certainly be a retreat from reality.

In light of the other things we know about Jesus, it's hard to imagine that he was mentally disturbed. Here is a man who spoke some of the most profound sayings ever recorded. His instructions have liberated many individuals in mental bondage. Clark H. Pinnock asks: "Was he deluded about his greatness, a paranoid, an unintentional deceiver, a schizophrenic? Again, the skill and depth of his teachings support the case only for his total mental soundness. If only we were as sane as he!"[8] A student at a California university told me that his psychology professor had said in class that "all he has to do is pick up the Bible and read portions of Christ's teaching to many of his patients. That's all the counseling they need."

Psychiatrist J. T. Fisher states: "If you were to take the sum total of all authoritative articles ever written by the most qualified of psychologists and psychiatrists on the subject of mental hygiene—if you were to combine them and refine them and cleave out the excess verbiage—if you were to take the whole of the meat and none of the parsley, and if you were to have these unadulterated bits of pure scientific knowledge concisely expressed by the most capable of living poets, you would have an awkward and incomplete summation of the Sermon on the Mount. And it would suffer immeasurably through comparison. For nearly two thousand years the Christian world has been holding in its hands the complete answer to its restless and fruitless yearnings. Here . . . rests the blueprint for successful human life with optimism, mental health, and contentment."[9]

C. S. Lewis writes: "The historical difficulty of giving for the life, sayings and influence of Jesus any explanation that is not harder than the Christian explanation is very great. The discrepancy between the depth and sanity . . . of His moral teaching and the rampant megalomania which must lie behind His theological teaching unless He is indeed God has never been satisfactorily explained. Hence the non-Christian hypotheses succeed one another with the restless fertility of bewilderment."[10]

Philip Schaff reasons: "Is such an intellect—clear as the sky, bracing as the mountain air, sharp and penetrating as a sword, thoroughly healthy and vigorous, always ready and always self-possessed—liable to a radical and most serious delusion concerning his own character and mission? Preposterous imagination!"[6]

WAS HE LORD?

I cannot personally conclude that Jesus was a liar or a lunatic. The only other alternative is that he was the Christ, the Son of God, as he claimed.

When I discuss this with most Jewish people, it's interesting how they respond. They usually tell me that Jesus was a moral, upright, religious leader, a good man, or some kind of prophet. I then share with them the claims Jesus made about himself and then the material in this chapter on the trilemma (liar, lunatic, or Lord). When I ask if they believe Jesus was a liar, there is a sharp "No!" Then I ask, "Do you believe he was a lunatic?" The reply is "Of course not." "Do you believe he is God?" Before I can get a breath in edgewise, there is a resounding "Absolutely not." Yet one has only so many choices.

The issue with these three alternatives is not

which is possible, for it is obvious that all three are possible. But rather, the question is "Which is more probable?" Who you decide Jesus Christ is must not be an idle intellectual exercise. You cannot put him on the shelf as a great moral teacher. That is not a valid option. He is either a liar, a lunatic, or Lord and God. You must make a choice. "But," as the Apostle John wrote, "these have been written that you may believe that Jesus is the Christ, the Son of God; and"—more important—"that believing you might have life in His name" (John 20:31).

The evidence is clearly in favor of Jesus as Lord. Some people, however, reject this clear evidence because of moral implications involved. They don't want to face up to the responsibility or implications of calling him Lord.

NOTES ON CHAPTER 2

1. C. S. Lewis, *Mere Christianity* (New York: The MacMillan Company, 1960), pp. 40–41.
2. F. J. A. Hort, *Way, Truth, and the Life* (New York: MacMillan and Co., 1894), p. 207.
3. Kenneth Scott Latourette, *A History of Christianity* (New York: Harper and Row, 1953), pp. 44, 48.
4. William E. Lecky, *History of European Morals from Augustus to Charlemagne* (New York: D. Appleton and Co., 1903), Vol. 2, pp. 8, 9.
5. Philip Schaff, *History of the Christian Church* (Grand Rapids: William B. Eerdmans Publishing Co., 1962). (Reprint from original 1910), p. 109.

6. Philip Schaff, *The Person of Christ* (New York: American Tract Society, 1913), pp. 94–95; p. 97.

7. Arthur P. Noyes, and Lawrence C. Kolb, *Modern Clinical Psychiatry* (Philadelphia: Saunders, 1958). (5th ed.)

8. Clark H. Pinnock, *Set Forth Your Case* (New Jersey: The Craig Press, 1967), p. 62.

9. J. T. Fisher, and L. S. Hawley, *A Few Buttons Missing* (Philadelphia: Lippincott, 1951), p. 273.

10. C. S. Lewis, *Miracles: A Preliminary Study* (New York: The MacMillan Company, 1947), p. 113.

3

What About Science?

Many people try to put off personal commitment to Christ by voicing the assumption that if you cannot prove something scientifically, it is not true or worthy of acceptance. Since one cannot prove scientifically the deity of Jesus or the resurrection, then twentieth-century individuals should know better than to accept Christ as Savior or to believe in the resurrection.

Often in a philosophy or history class I am confronted with the challenge, "Can you prove it scientifically?" I usually say, "Well, no, I'm not a scientist." Then you can hear the class chuckle and usually several voices can be heard saying, "Don't talk to me about it," or "See, you must take it all by faith" (meaning blind faith).

Recently on a flight to Boston I was talking with

the passenger next to me about why I personally
believe Christ is who he claimed to be. The pilot,
making his public relations rounds greeting the
passengers, overheard part of our conversation.
"You have a problem," he said. "What is that?" I
asked. "You can't prove it scientifically," he replied.

The mentality that modern humanity has descended to is amazing. Somehow, here in the
twentieth century we have so many who hold to
the opinion that if you can't prove it scientifically,
it's not true. Well, *that* is not true! There's a
problem of proving anything about a person or
event in history. We need to understand the
difference between scientific proof and what I call
legal-historical proof. Let me explain these two.

Scientific proof is based on showing that something is a fact by repeating the event in the
presence of the person questioning the fact. There
is a controlled environment where observations
can be made, data drawn, and hypotheses empirically verified.

The "scientific method, however it is defined, is
related to measurement of phenomena and experimentation or repeated observation."[1] Dr. James B.
Conant, former president of Harvard, writes: "Science is an interconnected series of concepts and
conceptual schemes that have developed as a
result of experimentation and observation, and
are fruitful of further experimentation and observations."[2]

Testing the truth of a hypothesis by the use of controlled experiments is one of the key techniques of the modern scientific method. For example, somebody says, "Ivory soap doesn't float." So I take the person to the kitchen, put eight inches of water in the sink at 82.7°, and drop in the soap. Plunk. Observations are made, data are drawn, and a hypothesis is empirically verified: Ivory soap floats.

Now if the scientific method was the only method of proving something, you couldn't prove that you went to your first hour class this morning or that you had lunch today. There's no way you can repeat those events in a controlled situation.

Now here's what is called the legal-historical proof, which is based on showing that something is fact beyond a reasonable doubt. In other words, a verdict is reached on the basis of the weight of the evidence. That is, there's no reasonable basis for doubting the decision. It depends upon three types of testimony: oral testimony, written testimony, and exhibits (such as a gun, bullet, notebook). Using the legal method of determining what happened, you could pretty well prove beyond a reasonable doubt that you were in class this morning: your friends saw you, you have your notes, the professor remembers you.

The scientific method can be used only to prove repeatable things; it isn't adequate for proving or disproving many questions about a person or event in history. The scientific method isn't appropriate for answering such questions as "Did George Washington live?" "Was Martin Luther King a civil rights leader?" "Who was Jesus of Nazareth?" "Was Robert Kennedy attorney general of the U.S.A.?" "Was Jesus Christ raised from the dead?" These are out of the realm of scientific proof, and we need to put them in the realm of legal proof. In other words, the scientific method, which is based on observation, the gathering of data, hypothesizing, deduction, and experimental verification to find and explain empirical regularities in nature, doesn't have the final answers to such questions as "Can you prove the resurrection?" or "Can you prove that Jesus is the Son of God?" When men and women rely upon the legal-historical method, they need to check out the reliability of the testimonies.

One thing that has especially appealed to me is that the Christian faith is not a blind, ignorant belief but rather an intelligent faith. Every time in the Bible when a person is called upon to exercise faith, it's an intelligent faith. Jesus said in John 8, "You shall know the truth," not ignore it. Christ was asked, "What is the greatest commandment of all?" He said, "To love the Lord your God with all your heart and all your mind." The problem with most people is that they seem to stop with their hearts. The facts about Christ never get to their minds. We've been given a mind innovated by the Holy Spirit to know God, as well as a heart to love him and a will to choose him. We need to function in all three areas to have a maximum relationship with God and to glorify him. I don't know about the reader, but my heart can't rejoice in what my mind has rejected. My heart and mind were created to work in harmony together. Never has an individual been called upon to commit intellectual suicide in trusting Christ as Savior and Lord.

In the next four chapters we will take a look at the evidence for the reliability of the written documents and for the credibility of the oral testimony and eyewitness accounts of Jesus.

NOTES ON CHAPTER 3

1. *The New Encyclopaedia Britannica*, Micropaedia Vol. VIII, p. 985.
2. James B. Conant, *Science and Common Sense* (New Haven: Yale University Press, 1951), p. 25.

4

Are the Biblical Records Reliable?

The New Testament provides the primary historical source for information about Jesus. Because of this, many critics during the nineteenth and twentieth centuries have attacked the reliability of the biblical documents. There seems to be a constant barrage of accusations that have no historical foundation or that have now been outdated by archaeological discoveries and research.

While I was lecturing at Arizona State University, a professor who had brought his literature class with him approached me after a "free-speech" lecture outdoors. He said, "Mr. McDowell, you are basing all your claims about Christ on a second-century document that is obsolete. I showed in class today how the New Testament was written so long after Christ that it could not be accurate in what it recorded.''

I replied, ''Your opinions or conclusions about the New Testament are twenty-five years out of date.''

That professor's opinions about the records concerning Jesus found their source in the conclusions of a German critic, F. C. Baur. Baur assumed that most of the New Testament Scriptures were not written until late in the second century A.D. He concluded that these writings came basically from myths or legends that had developed during the lengthy interval between the lifetime of Jesus and the time these accounts were set down in writing.

By the twentieth century, however, archaeological discoveries had confirmed the accuracy of the New Testament manuscripts. Discoveries of early papyri manuscripts (the John Ryland manuscript, A.D. 130; the Chester Beatty Papyri, A.D. 155; and the Bodmer Papyri II, A.D. 200) bridged the gap between the time of Christ and existing manuscripts from a later date.

Millar Burrows of Yale says: ''Another result of comparing New Testament Greek with the language of the papyri [discoveries] is an increase of confidence in the accurate transmission of the text of the New Testament itself.''[1] Such findings as these have increased scholarly confidence in the reliability of the Bible.

William Albright, who was the world's foremost biblical archaeologist, writes: "We can already say emphatically that there is no longer any solid basis for dating any book of the New Testament after about A.D. 80, two full generations before the date between 130 and 150 given by the more radical New Testament critics of today."[2] He reiterates this view in an interview for *Christianity Today*: "In my opinion, every book of the New Testament was written by a baptized Jew between the forties and the eighties of the first century A.D. (very probably sometime between about A.D. 50 and 75)."[3]

Sir William Ramsay is regarded as one of the greatest archaeologists ever to have lived. He was a student of the German historical school that taught that the Book of Acts was a product of the mid-second century A.D. and not the first century as it purports to be. After reading modern criticism about the Book of Acts, he became convinced that it was not a trustworthy account of the facts of that time (A.D. 50) and therefore was unworthy of consideration by a historian. So in his research on the history of Asia Minor, Ramsay paid little attention to the New Testament. His investigation, however, eventually compelled him to consider the writings of Luke. He observed the meticulous accuracy of the historical details, and gradually his attitude toward the Book of Acts began to change. He was forced to conclude that "Luke is a historian of the first rank . . . this author should be placed along with the very greatest of historians."[4] Because of the accuracy of the most minute detail, Ramsay finally conceded that Acts could not be a second-century document but was rather a mid-first-century account.

Many of the liberal scholars are being forced to consider earlier dates for the New Testament. Dr. John A. T. Robinson's conclusions in his new book *Redating the New Testament* are startlingly radical. His research led to the conviction that the whole of the New Testament was written before the Fall of Jerusalem in A.D. 70.[5]

Today the Form Critics say that the material was passed by word of mouth until it was written down in the form of the Gospels. Even though the period was much shorter than previously believed, they conclude that the Gospel accounts took on the forms of folk literature (legends, tales, myths, and parables).

One of the major criticisms against the Form Critics' idea of oral tradition development is that the period of oral tradition (as defined by the critics) is not long enough to have allowed the alterations in the tradition that these critics have alleged. Speaking of the brevity of the time element involved in the writing of the New Testament, Simon Kistemaker, professor of Bible at Dordt College, writes: "Normally, the accumulation of folklore among people of primitive culture takes many generations; it is a gradual process spread over centuries of time. But in conformity with the thinking of the form critic, we must conclude that the Gospel stories were produced and collected within little more than one generation. In terms of the form-critical approach, the formation of the individual Gospel units must be understood as a telescoped project with accelerated course of action."[6]

A. H. McNeile, former Regius Professor of Divinity at the University of Dublin, challenges Form Criticism's concept of oral tradition. He points out that Form Critics do not deal with the tradition of Jesus' words as closely as they should. A careful look at 1 Corinthians 7:10, 12, 25 shows the careful preservation and the existence of a genuine tradition of recording these words. In the Jewish religion it was customary for a student to memorize a rabbi's teaching. A good pupil was like "a plastered cistern that loses not a drop" (Mishna, Aboth, ii, 8). If we rely on C. F. Burney's theory (in *The Poetry of Our Lord*, 1925), we can assume that much of the Lord's teaching is in Aramaic poetical form, making it easy to be memorized.[7]

Paul L. Maier, professor of ancient history at Western Michigan University, writes: "Arguments that Christianity hatched its Easter myth over a lengthy period of time or that the sources were written many years after the event are simply not factual."[8] Analyzing Form Criticism, Albright wrote: "Only modern scholars who lack both historical method and perspective can spin such a web of speculation as that with which form

45

critics have surrounded the Gospel tradition." Albright's own conclusion was that "a period of twenty to fifty years is too slight to permit of any appreciable corruption of the essential content and even of the specific wording of the sayings of Jesus."[9]

Often when I am talking with someone about the Bible they sarcastically reply that you can't trust what the Bible says. Why, it was written almost 2,000 years ago. It's full of errors and discrepancies. I reply that I believe I *can* trust the Scriptures. Then I describe an incident that took place during a lecture in a history class. I made the statement that I believed there was more evidence for the reliability of the New Testament than for almost any ten pieces of classical literature put together. The professor sat over in the corner snickering, as if to say, "Oh, gee—come on." I said, "What are you snickering about?" He said, "The audacity to make the statement in a history class that the New Testament is reliable. That's ridiculous." Well, I appreciate it when somebody makes a statement like that because I always like to ask this one question. (I've never had a positive response.) I said, "Tell me, sir, as a historian, what are the tests that you apply to any piece of literature of history to determine if it's accurate or reliable?" The amazing thing was he didn't have any tests. I answered, "I have some tests." I believe that the historical reliability of the Scripture should be tested by the same criteria that all historical documents are tested by. Military historian C. Sanders lists and explains the three basic principles of historiography. They are the bibliographical test, the internal evidence test, and the external evidence test.[10]

BIBLIOGRAPHICAL TEST

The bibliographical test is an examination of the textual transmission by which documents reach us. In other words, not having the original documents, how reliable are the copies we have in regard to the number of manuscripts (MSS) and the time interval between the original and extant copy?

We can appreciate the tremendous wealth of manuscript authority of the New Testament by comparing it with textual material from other notable ancient sources.

The history of Thucydides (460-400 B.C.) is available to us from just eight MSS dated about A.D. 900, almost 1,300 years after he wrote. The MSS of the history of Herodotus are likewise late and scarce, and yet, as F. F. Bruce concludes, "No classical scholar would listen to an argument that the authenticity of Herodotus or Thucydides is in doubt because the earliest manuscripts of their works which are of use to us are over 1,300 years later than the originals."[11]

Aristotle wrote his poetics around 343 B.C. and

yet the earliest copy we have is dated A.D. 1100, nearly a 1,400-year gap, and only five MSS are in existence.

Caesar composed his history of the Gallic Wars between 58 and 50 B.C. and its manuscript authority rests on nine or ten copies dating 1,000 years after his death.

When it comes to the manuscript authority of the New Testament, the abundance of material is almost embarrassing in contrast. After the early papyri manuscript discoveries that bridged the gap between the times of Christ and the second century, an abundance of other MSS came to light. Over 20,000 copies of New Testament manuscripts are in existence today. The *Iliad* has 643 MSS and is second in manuscript authority after the New Testament.

Sir Frederic Kenyon, who was the director and principal librarian at the British Museum and second to none in authority in issuing statements about manuscripts, concludes: "The interval then between the dates of original composition and the earliest extant evidence becomes so small as to be in fact negligible, and the last foundation for any doubt that the Scriptures have come down to us substantially as they were written has now been removed. Both the authenticity and the general integrity of the books of the New Testament may be regarded as finally established."[12]

The New Testament Greek scholar J. Harold Greenlee adds: "Since scholars accept as generally trustworthy the writings of the ancient classics even though the earliest MSS were written so long after the original writings and the number of extant MSS is in many instances so small, it is clear that the reliability of the text of the New Testament is likewise assured."[13]

The application of the bibliographical test to the New Testament assures us that it has more manuscript authority than any piece of literature from antiquity. Adding to that authority the more than 100 years of intensive New Testament textual criticism, one can conclude that an authentic New Testament text has been established.

INTERNAL EVIDENCE TEST

The bibliographical test has determined only that the text we have now is what was originally recorded. One has still to determine whether that written record is credible and to what extent. That is the problem of internal criticism, which is the second test of historicity listed by C. Sanders.

At this point the literary critic still follows Aristotle's dictum: "The benefit of the doubt is to be given to the document itself, and not arrogated by the critic to himself." In other words, as John W. Montgomery summarizes: "One must listen to the claims of the document under analysis, and not assume fraud or error unless the author disqualified himself by contradictions or known factual inaccuracies."[14]

Dr. Louis Gottschalk, former professor of history at the University of Chicago, outlines his historical method in a guide used by many for historical investigation. Gottschalk points out that the ability of the writer or the witness to tell the truth is helpful to the historian to determine credibility, "even if it is contained in a document obtained by force or fraud, or is otherwise impeachable, or is based on hearsay evidence, or is from an interested witness."[15]

This "ability to tell the truth" is closely related to the witness's nearness both geographically and chronologically to the events recorded. The New Testament accounts of the life and teaching of Jesus were recorded by men who had been either eyewitnesses themselves or who related the accounts of eyewitnesses of the actual events or teachings of Christ.

Luke 1:1–3—"Inasmuch as many have undertaken to compile an account of the things accomplished among us, just as those who from the beginning were eyewitnesses and servants of the Word have handed them down to us, it seemed fitting for me as well, having investigated everything carefully from the beginning, to write it out for you in consecutive order, most excellent Theophilus."

2 Peter 1:16—"For we did not follow cleverly devised tales when we made known to you the

power and coming of our Lord Jesus Christ, but we were eyewitnesses of His majesty."

1 John 1:3—". . . what we have seen and heard we proclaim to you also, that you also may have fellowship with us; and indeed our fellowship is with the Father, and with His Son Jesus Christ."

John 19:35—"And he who has seen has borne witness, and his witness is true; and he knows that he is telling the truth, so that you also may believe."

Luke 3:1—"Now in the fifteenth year of the reign of Tiberius Caesar, when Pontius Pilate was governor of Judea, and Herod was tetrarch of Galilee, and his brother Phillip was tetrarch of the region of Ituraea and Trachonitis, and Lysanias was tetrarch of Abilene. . . ."

This closeness to the recorded accounts is an extremely effective means of certifying the accuracy of what is retained by a witness. The historian, however, also has to deal with the eyewitness who consciously or unconsciously tells falsehoods even though he is near to the event and is competent to tell the truth.

The New Testament accounts of Christ were being circulated within the lifetimes of those alive at the time of his life. These people could certainly confirm or deny the accuracy of the accounts. In advocating their case for the gospel, the apostles had appealed (even when confronting their most severe opponents) to common knowledge concerning Jesus. They not only said, "Look, we saw this" or "We heard that . . ." but they turned the tables around and right in front of adverse critics said, "You also know about these things. . . . You saw them; you yourselves know about it." One had better be careful when he says to his opposition, "You know this also," because if he isn't right in the details, it will be shoved right back down his throat.

Acts 2:22—"Men of Israel, listen to these words: Jesus the Nazarene, a man attested to you by God with miracles and wonders and signs which God performed through Him in your midst, just as you yourselves know . . ."

Acts 26:24–28—"And while Paul was saying this in his defense, Festus said in a loud voice, 'Paul, you are out of your mind! Your great learning is driving you mad.' But Paul said, 'I am not out of my mind, most excellent Festus, but I utter words of sober truth. For the king knows about these matters, and I speak to him also with confidence, since I am persuaded that none of these things escape his notice; for this has not been done in a corner.'"

Concerning the primary-source value of the New Testament records, F. F. Bruce, Rylands Professor of Biblical Criticism and Exegesis at the University of Manchester, says: "And it was not only friendly eyewitnesses that the early preachers had to reckon with; there were others less well disposed who were also conversant with the main facts of the ministry and death of Jesus. The disciples could not afford to risk inaccuracies (not to speak of willful manipulation of the facts), which would at once be exposed by those who would be only too glad to do so. On the contrary, one of the strong points in the original apostolic preaching is the confident appeal to the knowledge of the hearers; they not only said, 'We are witnesses of these things,' but also, 'As you yourselves also know' (Acts 2:22). Had there been any tendency to depart from the facts in any material respect, the possible presence of hostile witnesses in the audience would have served as a further corrective."[11]

Lawrence J. McGinley of Saint Peter's College comments on the value of hostile witnesses in relationship to recorded events: "First of all, eyewitnesses of the events in question were still alive when the tradition had been completely formed; and among those eyewitnesses were bitter enemies of the new religious movement. Yet the tradition claimed to narrate a series of well-known deeds and publicly taught doctrines at a time when false statements could, and would, be challenged."[16]

New Testament scholar Robert Grant of the University of Chicago concludes: "At the time they [the synoptic gospels] were written or may be supposed to have been written, there were eyewitnesses and their testimony was not completely disregarded. . . . This means that the gospels must be regarded as largely reliable witnesses to the life, death, and resurrection of Jesus."[17]

53

Will Durant, who was trained in the discipline of historical investigation and spent his life analyzing records of antiquity, writes: "Despite the prejudices and theological preconceptions of the evangelists, they record many incidents that mere inventors would have concealed—the competition of the apostles for high places in the Kingdom, their flight after Jesus' arrest, Peter's denial, the failure of Christ to work miracles in Galilee, the references of some auditors to his possible insanity, his early uncertainty as to his mission, his confessions of ignorance as to the future, his moments of bitterness, his despairing cry on the cross; no one reading these scenes can doubt the reality of the figure behind them. That a few simple men should in one generation have invented so powerful and appealing a personality, so lofty an ethic, and so inspiring a vision of human brotherhood, would be a miracle far more incredible than any recorded in the Gospels. After two centuries of Higher Criticism the outlines of the life, character, and teaching of Christ remain reasonably clear, and constitute the most fascinating feature in the history of Western man."[18]

EXTERNAL EVIDENCE TEST

The third test of historicity is that of external evidence. The issue here is whether other historical material confirms or denies the internal testimony of the documents themselves. In other words, what sources are there, apart from the literature under analysis, that substantiate its accuracy, reliability, and authenticity?

Gottschalk argues that "*conformity* or *agreement* with other known historical or scientific facts is often the decisive test of evidence, whether of one or of more witnesses."[15]

Two friends of the Apostle John confirm the internal evidence from John's accounts. The historian Eusebius preserves writings of Papias, bishop of Hierapolis (A.D. 130): "The Elder [Apostle John] used to say this also: 'Mark, having been the interpreter of Peter, wrote down accurately all that he [Peter] mentioned, whether sayings or doings of Christ, not, however, in order. For he was neither a hearer nor a companion of the Lord; but afterwards, as I said, he accompanied Peter, who adapted his teachings as necessity required, not as though he were making a compilation of the sayings of the Lord. So then Mark made no mistake, writing down in this way some things as he mentioned them; for he paid attention to this one thing, not to omit anything that he had heard, not to include any false statement among them.' "[19]

Irenaeus, Bishop of Lyons (A.D. 180. Irenaeus was a student of Polycarp, Bishop of Smyrna, who had been a Christian for eighty-six years, and was a disciple of John the Apostle) wrote: "Matthew published his Gospel among the Hebrews [i.e.,

Jews] in their own tongue, when Peter and Paul were preaching the gospel in Rome and founding the church there. After their departure [i.e., death, which strong tradition places at the time of the Neronian persecution in 64], Mark, the disciple and interpreter of Peter, himself handed down to us in writing the substance of Peter's preaching. Luke, the follower of Paul, set down in a book the gospel preached by his teacher. Then John, the disciple of the Lord, who also leaned on his breast [this is a reference to John 13:25 and 21:20], himself produced his Gospel, while he was living at Ephesus in Asia."[20]

Archaeology often provides powerful external evidence. It contributes to biblical criticism, not in the area of inspiration and revelation, but by providing evidence of accuracy about events that are recorded. Archaeologist Joseph Free writes: "Archaeology has confirmed countless passages which have been rejected by critics as unhistorical or contradictory to known facts."[21]

We have already seen how archaeology caused Sir William Ramsay to change his initial negative convictions about the historicity of Luke and come to the conclusion that the Book of Acts was accurate in its description of the geography, antiquities, and society of Asia Minor.

F. F. Bruce notes that "where Luke has been suspected of inaccuracy, and accuracy has been vindicated by some inscriptional [external] evidence, it may be legitimate to say that archaeology has confirmed the New Testament record."[22]

A. N. Sherwin-White, a classical historian, writes that "for Acts the confirmation of historicity is overwhelming." He continues by saying that "any attempt to reject its basic historicity even in matters of detail must now appear absurd. Roman historians have long taken it for granted."[23]

After personally trying to shatter the historicity and validity of the Scriptures, I have come to the conclusion that they are historically trustworthy. If a person discards the Bible as unreliable in this sense, then he or she must discard almost all the literature of antiquity. One problem I constantly face is the desire on the part of many to apply one standard or test to secular literature and another to the Bible. We need to apply the same test, whether the literature under investigation is secular or religious. Having done this, I believe we can say, "The Bible is trustworthy and historically reliable in its witness about Jesus."

Dr. Clark H. Pinnock, professor of systematic theology at Regent College, states: "There exists no document from the ancient world witnessed by so excellent a set of textual and historical testimonies, and offering so superb an array of historical data on which an intelligent decision may be made. An honest [person] cannot dismiss a source of this kind. Skepticism regarding the historical credentials of Christianity is based upon an irrational [i.e., antisupernatural] bias."[24]

NOTES ON CHAPTER 4

1. Millar Burrows, *What Mean These Stones*. (New York: Meridian Books, 1956), p. 52.
2. William F. Albright, *Recent Discoveries in Bible Lands* . (New York: Funk and Wagnalls, 1955), p. 136.
3. William F. Albright, *Christianity Today*, Vol. 7, Jan. 18, 1963, p. 3.
4. Sir William Ramsay, *The Bearing of Recent Discovery on the Trustworthiness of the New Testament*. (London: Hodder and Stoughton, 1915), p. 222.
5. John A. T. Robinson, *Redating the New Testament* (London: SCM Press, 1976).
6. Simon Kistenmaker, *The Gospels in Current Study*. (Grand Rapids: Baker Book House, 1972), pp. 48–49.
7. A. H. McNeile, *An Introduction to the Study of the New Testament*. (London: Oxford University Press, 1953), p. 54.
8. Paul L. Maier, *First Easter: The True and Unfamiliar Story*. (New York: Harper and Row, 1973), p. 122.
9. William F. Albright, *From the Stone Age to Christianity* (second edition). (Baltimore: John Hopkins Press, 1946), pp. 297, 298.
10. C. Sanders, *Introduction to Research in English Literary History*. (New York: MacMillan Company, 1952), pp. 143 ff..
11. F. F. Bruce, *The New Testament Documents: Are They Reliable?* (Downers Grove, Ill. 60515: Inter Varsity Press, 1964), pp. 16 f.; p. 33.
12. Sir Frederic Kenyon, *The Bible and Archaeology*. (New York: Harper and Row, 1940), pp. 288, 289.
13. J. Harold Greenlee, *Introduction to New Testament Textual Criticism* (Grand Rapids: William B. Eerdmans Publishing Company, 1964), p. 16.
14. John Warwick Montgomery, *History and Christianity* (Downers Grove, Ill.: InterVarsity Press, 1971), p. 29.
15. Louis R. Gottschalk, *Understanding History* (New York: Knopf, 1969, 2nd ed), p. 150; p. 161; p. 168.

16. Lawrence J. McGinley, *Form Criticism of the Synoptic Healing Narratives* (Woodstock, Maryland: Woodstock College Press, 1944), p. 25.

17. Robert Grant, *Historical Introduction to the New Testament* (New York: Harper and Row, 1963), p. 302.

18. Will Durant, *Caesar and Christ,* in *The Story of Civilization,* Vol. 3. (New York: Simon & Schuster, 1944), p. 557.

19. Eusebius. *Ecclesiastical History,* Book 3, Chapter 39.

20. Irenaeus. *Against Heresies.* 3.1.1.

21. Joseph Free, *Archaeology and Bible History* (Wheaton, Ill: Scripture Press, 1969), p. 1.

22. F. F. Bruce, "Archaeological Confirmation of the New Testament," in *Revelation and the Bible.* Edited by Carl Henry. (Grand Rapids: Baker Book House, 1969), p. 331.

23. A. N. Sherwin-White, *Roman Society and Roman Law in the New Testament* (Oxford: Clarendon Press, 1963), p. 189.

24. Clark Pinnock, *Set Forth Your Case* (New Jersey: The Craig Press, 1968), p. 58.

5

Who Would Die for a Lie?

One area often overlooked in challenges to Christianity is the transformation of Jesus' apostles. Their changed lives provide solid testimony for the validity of his claims. Since the Christian faith is historical, to investigate it we must rely heavily upon testimony, both written and oral.

There are many definitions of "history," but the one I prefer is "a knowledge of the past based upon testimony." If someone says, "I don't believe that's a good definition," I ask, "Do you believe that Napoleon lived?" They almost always reply, "Yes." "Have you seen him?" I ask, and they confess they haven't. "How do you know, then?" Well, they are relying on testimony.

This definition of history has one inherent problem. The testimony must be reliable or the hearer will be misinformed. Christianity involves knowledge of the past based upon testimony, so now we must ask, "Were the original oral testimonies about Jesus trustworthy? Can they be trusted to have conveyed correctly what Jesus said and did?" I believe they can be.

I can trust the apostles' testimonies because, of those twelve men, eleven died martyrs' deaths on the basis of two things: the resurrection of Christ, and their belief in him as the Son of God. They were tortured and flogged, and they finally faced death by some of the cruelest methods then known:

1) Peter—crucified
2) Andrew—crucified
3) Matthew—the sword
4) John—natural
5) James, son of Alphaeus—crucified
6) Philip—crucified
7) Simon—crucified
8) Thaddaeus—killed by arrows
9) James, brother of Jesus—stoned
10) Thomas—spear thrust
11) Bartholomew—crucified
12) James, son of Zebedee—the sword

The response that is usually chorused back is this: "Why, a lot of people have died for a lie; so what does it prove?"

Yes, a lot of people have died for a lie, but they

thought it was the truth. Now if the resurrection didn't take place (i.e., was false), the disciples knew it. I find no way to demonstrate that they could have been deceived. Therefore these eleven men not only died for a lie—here is the catch—but they knew it was a lie. It would be hard to find eleven people in history who died for a lie, knowing it was a lie.

We need to be cognizant of several factors in order to appreciate what they did. First, when the apostles wrote or spoke, they did so as eyewitnesses of the events they described.

Peter said: "For we did not follow cleverly devised tales when we made known to you the power and coming of our Lord Jesus Christ, but we were eyewitnesses of his majesty" (2 Peter 1:16). The apostles certainly knew the difference between myth or legend and reality.

John emphasized the eyewitness aspect of the Jews' knowledge: "What was from the beginning, what we have heard, what we have seen with our eyes, what we beheld and our hands handled, concerning the Word of life—and the life was manifested, and we have seen and bear witness and proclaim to you the eternal life, which was with the Father and was manifested to us—what we have seen and heard we proclaim to you also, that you also may have fellowship with us; and indeed our fellowship is with the Father, and with His Son Jesus Christ" (1 John 1:1–3).

Luke said: "Inasmuch as many have undertaken

to compile an account of the things accomplished among us, just as those who from the beginning were eyewitnesses and servants of the Word have handed them down to us, it seemed fitting for me as well, having investigated everything carefully from the beginning, to write it out for you in consecutive order" (Luke 1:1–3).

Then in the book of Acts, Luke described the forty-day period after the resurrection when his followers closely observed him: "The first account I composed . . . about all that Jesus began to do and teach, until the day when He was taken up, after He had by the Holy Spirit given orders to the apostles whom He had chosen. To these He also presented Himself alive, after His suffering, by many convincing proofs, appearing to them over a period of forty days, and speaking of the things concerning the kingdom of God" (Acts 1:1–3).

John began the last portion of his Gospel by saying that there were "many other signs therefore Jesus also performed in the presence of the disciples, which are not written in this book" (John 20:30).

The main content of these eyewitness testimonies concerned the resurrection. The apostles were witnesses of his resurrected life:

Luke 24:48	Acts 3:15
John 15:27	Acts 4:33
Acts 1:8	Acts 5:32
Acts 2:24, 32	Acts 10:39

Acts 10:41	1 John 1:2
Acts 13:31	Acts 22:15
1 Corinthians 15:4–9	Acts 23:11
1 Corinthians 15:15	Acts 26:16

Second, the apostles themselves had to be convinced that Jesus was raised from the dead. At first they hadn't believed. They went and hid (Mark 14:50). They didn't hesitate to express their doubts. Only after ample and convincing evidence did they believe. There was Thomas, who said he wouldn't believe that Christ was raised from the dead until he had put his finger in the nail prints. Thomas later died a martyr's death for Christ. Was he deceived? He bet his life he wasn't.

Then there was Peter. He denied Christ several times during his trial. Finally he deserted Jesus. But something happened to this coward. Just a short time after Christ's crucifixion and burial, Peter showed up in Jerusalem preaching boldly, at the threat of death, that Jesus was the Christ and had been resurrected. Finally Peter was crucified upside down. Was he deceived? What had happened to him? What had transformed him so dramatically into a bold lion for Jesus? Why was he willing to die for him? The only explanation I am satisfied with is 1 Corinthians 15:5—"and then He appeared to Cephas [Peter]" (John 1:42).

The classic example of a man convinced against his will was James, the brother of Jesus (Matthew 13:55; Mark 6:3). Although James wasn't one of the original twelve (Matthew 10:2–4), he was later recognized as an apostle (Galatians 1:19), as were Paul and Barnabas (Acts 14:14). When Jesus was alive, James didn't believe in his brother Jesus as the Son of God (John 7:5). He as well as his brothers and sisters may even have mocked him. "You want people to believe in you? Why don't you go up to Jerusalem and do your thing?" For James it must have been humiliating for Jesus to go around and bring ridicule to the family name by his wild claims ("I am the way, and the truth, and the life; no one comes to the Father, but through Me"—John 14:6; "I am the vine, you are the branches"—John 15:5; "I am the good shepherd . . . and My own know Me"—John 10:14). What would *you* think if your brother said such things?

But something happened to James. After Jesus was crucified and buried, James was preaching in Jerusalem. His message was that Jesus died for sins and was resurrected and is alive. Eventually James became one of the leaders of the Jerusalem church and wrote a book, the epistle of James. He began it by writing, "James, a servant of God and of the Lord Jesus Christ." His brother. Eventually James died a martyr's death by stoning at the hands of Ananias the high priest (Josephus). Was James deceived? No, the only plausible explanation is 1 Corinthians 15:7—"then He appeared to James."

If the resurrection was a lie, the apostles knew

it. Were they perpetuating a colossal hoax? That possibility is inconsistent with what we know about the moral quality of their lives. They personally condemned lying and stressed honesty. They encouraged people to know the truth. The historian Edward Gibbon in his famous work, *The History of the Decline and Fall of the Roman Empire*, gives the "purer but austere morality of the first Christians" as one of five reasons for the rapid success of Christianity. Michael Green, principal of St. John's College, Nottingham, observes that the resurrection "was the belief that turned heartbroken followers of a crucified rabbi into the courageous witnesses and martyrs of the early church. This was the one belief that separated the followers of Jesus from the Jews and turned them into the community of the resurrection. You could imprison them, flog them, kill them, but you could not make them deny their conviction that 'on the third day he rose again.'"[1]

Third, the bold conduct of the apostles immediately after they were convinced of the resurrection makes it unlikely that it all was a fraud. They became bold almost overnight. Peter who had denied Christ stood up even at the threat of death and proclaimed Jesus alive after the resurrection. The authorities arrested the followers of Christ and beat them, yet they soon would be back in the street speaking out about Jesus (Acts 5:40–42). Their friends noticed their buoyancy and their enemies noticed their courage. Nor did they preach in an obscure town, but in Jerusalem.

Jesus' followers couldn't have faced torture and death unless they were convinced of his resurrection. The unanimity of their message and course of conduct was amazing. The chances against any large group being in agreement is enormous, yet they all agreed on the truth of the resurrection. If they were deceivers, it's hard to explain why one of them didn't break down under pressure.

Pascal, the French philosopher, writes: "The allegation that the Apostles were imposters is quite absurd. Let us follow the charge to its logical conclusion: Let us picture those twelve men, meeting after the death of Jesus Christ, and entering into conspiracy to say that He has risen. That would have constituted an attack upon both the civil and the religious authorities. The heart of man is strangely given to fickleness and change; it is swayed by promises, tempted by material things. If any one of those men had yielded to temptations so alluring, or given way to the more compelling arguments of prison, torture, they would have all been lost."[2]

"How have they turned, almost overnight," asks Michael Green, "into the indomitable band of enthusiasts who braved opposition, cynicism, ridicule, hardship, prison, and death in three continents, as they preached everywhere Jesus and the resurrection?"[3]

An unknown writer descriptively narrates the changes that occurred in the lives of the apostles:

"On the day of the crucifixion they were filled with sadness; on the first day of the week with gladness. At the crucifixion they were hopeless; on the first day of the week their hearts glowed with certainty and hope. When the message of the resurrection first came they were incredulous and hard to be convinced, but once they became assured they never doubted again. What could account for the astonishing change in these men in so short a time? The mere removal of the body from the grave could never have transformed their spirits and characters. Three days are not enough for a legend to spring up which would so affect them. Time is needed for a process of legendary growth. It is a psychological fact that demands a full explanation. Think of the character of the witnesses, men and women who gave the world the highest ethical teaching it has ever known, and who even on the testimony of their enemies lived it out in their lives. Think of the psychological absurdity of picturing a little band of defeated cowards cowering in an upper room one day and a few days later transformed into a company that no persecution could silence—and then attempting to attribute this dramatic change to nothing more convincing than a miserable fabrication they were trying to foist upon the world. That simply wouldn't make sense."

Kenneth Scott Latourette writes: "The effects of the resurrection and the coming of the Holy Spirit upon the disciples were . . . of major importance.

From discouraged, disillusioned men and women who sadly looked back upon the days when they had hoped that Jesus 'was he who should redeem Israel,' they were made over into a company of enthusiastic witnesses."[4]

Paul Little asks: "Are these men, who helped transform the moral structure of society, consummate liars or deluded madmen? These alternatives are harder to believe than the fact of the Resurrection, and there is no shred of evidence to support them."[5]

The steadfastness of the apostles even to death cannot be explained away. According to the *Encyclopaedia Britannica*, Origen records that Peter was crucified head downward. Herbert Workman describes Peter's death: "Thus Peter, as our Lord had prophesied, was 'girt' by another, and 'carried' out to die along the Aurelian Way, to a place hard by the gardens of Nero on the Vatican hill, where so many of his brethren had already suffered a cruel death. At his own request he was crucified head downwards, as unworthy to suffer like his Master."[6]

Harold Mattingly, in his history text, writes: "The apostles, St. Peter and St. Paul, sealed their witnesses with their blood."[7] Tertullian wrote that "no man would be willing to die unless he knew he had the truth."[8] Harvard law professor Simon Greenleaf, a man who lectured for years on how to break down a witness and determine whether or not a witness is lying, concludes: "The annals of military warfare afford scarcely an example of the like heroic constancy, patience, and unflinching courage. They had every possible motive to review carefully the grounds of their faith, and the evidences of the great facts and truths which they asserted."[9]

The apostles went through the test of death to substantiate the veracity of what they were proclaiming. I believe I can trust their testimony more than that of most people I meet today, people who aren't willing to walk across the street for what they believe, let alone die for it.

NOTES ON CHAPTER 5

1. Michael Green, "Editor's Preface" In George Eldon Ladd, *I Believe in the Resurrection of Jesus* (Grand Rapids: William B. Eerdmans Publishing Co., 1975).
2. Robert W. Gleason (Ed.), *The Essential Pascal*, Trans. by G. F. Pullen (New York: Mentor-Omega Books, 1966), p. 187.
3. Michael Green, *Man Alive!* (Downers Grove, Ill.: InterVarsity Press, 1968), pp. 23–24.
4. Kenneth Scott Latourette, *A History of Christianity* (New York: Harper and Brothers Publishers, 1937) Vol. I, p. 59.
5. Paul Little, *Know Why You Believe* (Wheaton, Ill: Scripture Press Publications, Inc., 1971), p. 63.
6. Herbert B. Workman, *The Martyrs of the Early Church* (London: Charles H. Kelly, 1913), pp. 18–19.
7. Harold Mattingly, *Roman Imperial Civilization* (London: Edward Arnold Publishers, Ltd., 1967), p. 226.
8. Gaston Foote, *The Transformation of the Twelve* (Nashville: Abingdon Press, 1958), p. 12.

9. Simon Greenleaf, *An Examination of the Testimony of the Four Evangelists by the Rules of Evidence Administered in the Courts of Justice* (Grand Rapids: Baker Book House, 1965. Reprint of 1874 edition. New York: J. Cockroft and Co.), p. 29.

6

What Good Is a Dead Messiah?

A lot of people have died for a good cause. Look at the student in San Diego who burned himself to death protesting against the Vietnam war. In the sixties many Buddhists burned themselves to death in order to bring world attention to Southeast Asia.

The problem with the apostles is that their good cause died on the cross. They believed Jesus to be the Messiah. They didn't think he could die. They were convinced that he was the one to set up the kingdom of God and to rule over the people of Israel.

In order to understand the apostles' relationship to Christ and to understand why the cross was so incomprehensible to them, you have to

grasp the attitude about the Messiah at the time of
Christ.

The life and teachings of Jesus were in tremendous conflict with the Jewish messianic speculation of that day. From childhood a Jew was taught
that when the Messiah came, he would be a
reigning, victorious, political leader. He would
release the Jews from bondage and restore Israel to
its rightful place. A suffering Messiah was "completely foreign to the Jewish conception of messiahship."[1]

E. F. Scott gives his account of the time of
Christ: ". . . the period was one of intense excite-
ment. The religious leaders found it almost impossible to restrain the ardour of the people, who
were waiting everywhere for the appearance of
the promised Deliverer. This mood of expectancy
had no doubt been heightened by the events of
recent history.

"For more than a generation past the Romans
had been encroaching on Jewish freedom, and
their measures of repression had stirred the spirit
of patriotism to fiercer life. The dream of a mirac-
ulous deliverance, and of a Messianic king who
would effect it, assumed a new meaning in that
critical time; but in itself it was nothing new.
Behind the ferment of which we have evidence in
the Gospels, we can discern a long period of
growing anticipation.

"To the people at large the Messiah remained
what he had been to Isaiah and his contempo-

raries—the Son of David who would bring victory and prosperity to the Jewish nation. In the light of the Gospel references it can hardly be doubted that the popular conception of the Messiah was mainly national and political."[2]

Jewish scholar Joseph Klausner writes: "The Messiah became more and more not only a preeminent political ruler but also a man of preeminent moral qualities."[3]

Jacob Gartenhus reflects the prevailing Jewish beliefs of the time of Christ: "The Jews awaited the Messiah as the one who would deliver them from Roman oppression . . . the messianic hope was basically for a national liberation."[4]

The *Jewish Encyclopaedia* states that the Jews "yearned for the promised deliverer of the house of David, who would free them from the yoke of the hated foreign usurper, would put an end to the impious Roman rule, and would establish His own reign of peace and justice in its place."[5]

At that time the Jews were taking refuge in the promised Messiah. The apostles held the same beliefs as the people around them. As Millar Burrows stated, "Jesus was so unlike what all Jews expected the son of David to be that His own disciples found it almost impossible to connect the idea of the Messiah with Him."[6] The grave communications by Jesus about being crucified were not at all welcomed by his disciples (Luke 9:22). There "seems to have been the hope," observes A. B. Bruce, "that He had taken too

74

gloomy a view of the situation, and that His apprehensions would turn out groundless . . . a crucified Christ was a scandal and a contradiction to the apostles; quite as much as it continued to be to the majority of the Jewish people after the Lord had ascended to glory."[7]

Alfred Edersheim, once Grinfield Lecturer on the Septuagint at Oxford, was right in concluding that "the most unlike thing to Christ were His times."[8]

One can detect in the New Testament the apostles' attitude toward Christ: their expectation of a reigning Messiah. After Jesus told his disciples that he had to go to Jerusalem and suffer, James and John asked him to promise that in his kingdom they could sit on his right and left hands (Mark 10:32–38). What type of Messiah were they thinking of? A suffering, crucified Messiah? No, a political ruler. Jesus indicated that they misunderstood what he had to do; they didn't know what they were asking. When Jesus predicted his suffering and crucifixion, the twelve apostles couldn't figure out what he meant (Luke 18:31–34). Because of their background and training they believed they were in on a good thing. Then came Calvary. All hopes departed of Jesus being their Messiah. Discouraged, they returned to their homes. All those years wasted.

Dr. George Eldon Ladd, professor of New Testament at Fuller Theological Seminary, writes: "This is also why his disciples forsook him when he was taken captive. Their minds were so completely imbued with the idea of a conquering Messiah whose role it was to subdue his enemies that when they saw him broken and bleeding under the scourging, a helpless prisoner in the hands of Pilate, and when they saw him led away, nailed to a cross to die as a common criminal, all their messianic hopes for Jesus were shattered. It is a sound psychological fact that we hear only what we are prepared to hear. Jesus' predictions of his suffering and death fell on deaf ears. The disciples, in spite of his warnings, were unprepared for it. . . ."[9]

But a few weeks after the crucifixion, in spite of their former doubts, the disciples were in Jerusalem proclaiming Jesus as Savior and Lord, the Messiah of the Jews. The only reasonable explanation that I can see of this change is 1 Corinthians 15:5—"He appeared . . . then to the twelve." What else could have caused the despondent disciples to go out and suffer and die for a crucified Messiah? He certainly must have "presented Himself alive, after His suffering, by many convincing proofs, appearing to them over a period of forty days" (Acts 1:3).

Yes, a lot of people have died for a good cause, but the good cause of the apostles died on the cross. Only the resurrection and resultant contact with Christ convinced his followers he was the Messiah. To this they testified not only with their lips and lives, but with their deaths.

NOTES ON CHAPTER 6

1. *Encyclopedia International*, 1972, Vol. 4, p. 407.
2. Ernest Findlay Scott, *Kingdom and the Messiah* (Edinburgh: T. & T. Clark, 1911), p. 55.
3. Joseph Klausner, *The Messianic Idea in Israel* (New York: The MacMillan Co., 1955), p. 23.
4. Jacob Gartenhaus, "The Jewish Conception of the Messiah," *Christianity Today*, March 13, 1970, pp. 8–10.
5. *The Jewish Encyclopaedia* (New York: Funk and Wagnalls Co., 1906), Vol. 8, p. 508.
6. Millar Burrows, *More Light on the Dead Sea Scrolls* (London: Secker & Warburg, 1958), p. 68.
7. A. B. Bruce, *The Training of the Twelve* (original 1894) (Grand Rapids: Kregel Publications, 1971), p. 177.
8. Alfred Edersheim, *Sketches of Jewish Social Life in the Days of Christ* (reprint edition; Grand Rapids: William B. Eerdmans Publishing Co., 1960), p. 29.
9. George Eldon Ladd, *I Believe in the Resurrection of Jesus* (Grand Rapids: William B. Eerdmans Publishing Co., 1975), p. 38.

7
Did You Hear What Happened to Saul?

Jack, a friend of mine who has spoken in many universities, was surprised one day when he arrived at a campus. He discovered that the students had arranged for him to have a public discussion that night with the "university atheist." His opponent was an eloquent philosophy professor who was extremely antagonistic to Christianity. Jack was to speak first. He discussed various proofs for the resurrection of Jesus, the conversion of the apostle Paul, and then gave his personal testimony about how Christ had changed his life when he was a university student.

When it was time for the professor to speak, he was very nervous. He couldn't refute the evidence for the resurrection, or Jack's personal testimony, so he turned to the subject of the Apostle Paul's radical conversion to Christianity. He used the line of argument that "people can often be so psychologically involved in what they're combating that they end up embracing it." At this point my friend smiled gently, and responded, "You'd better be careful, sir, or you're liable to become a Christian."

One of the most influential testimonies to Christianity was when Saul of Tarsus, perhaps Christianity's most rabid antagonist, became the Apostle Paul. Saul was a Hebrew zealot, a religious leader. Being born in Tarsus gave him the opportunity to be exposed to the most advanced learning of his day. Tarsus was a university city known for its Stoic philosophers and culture. Strabo, the Greek geographer, praised Tarsus for being so interested in education and philosophy.[1a]

Paul, like his father, possessed Roman citizenship, a high privilege. He seemed to be well versed in Hellenistic culture and thought. He had great command of the Greek language and displayed dialectic skill. He quoted from less familiar poets and philosophers:

Acts 17:28—"For in him we live and move and exist [Epimenides], as even some of your own poets have said, 'For we also are His offspring' [Aratus, Cleanthes]";

1 Corinthians 15:33—"Do not be deceived: 'Bad company corrupts good morals' [Menander]";

Titus 1:12—"One of themselves, a prophet of

their own, said, 'Cretans are always liars, evil beasts, lazy gluttons' [Epimenides].''

Paul's education was Jewish and took place under the strict doctrines of the Pharisees. At about age fourteen, he was sent to study under Gamaliel, one of the great rabbis of the time, the grandson of Hillel. Paul asserted that he was not only a Pharisee but the son of Pharisees (Acts 23:6). He could boast: "I was advancing in Judaism beyond many of my contemporaries among my countrymen, being more extremely zealous for my ancestral traditions" (Galatians 1:14).

If one is to understand Paul's conversion, it is necessary to see why he was so vehemently anti-Christian: the reason was his devotion to the Jewish law, which triggered his adamant discontent with Christ and the early church.

Paul's "offence with the Christian message was not," as Jacques Dupont writes, "with the affirmation of Jesus' messiahship [but] . . . with the attributing to Jesus of a saving role which robbed the law of all its value in the purpose of salvation. . . . [Paul was] violently hostile to the Christian faith because of the importance which he attached to the law as a way of salvation.''[2]

The Encyclopaedia Britannica states that the new sect of Judaism calling themselves Christians struck at the essence of Paul's Jewish training and rabbinic studies.[1b] To exterminate this sect became his passion (Galatians 1:13). So Paul began his pursuit to death of "the sect of the Nazarenes"

(Acts 26:9–11). He literally "laid waste the church" (Acts 8:3). He set out for Damascus with documents authorizing him to seize the followers of Jesus and bring them back to face trial.

Then something happened to Paul. "Now Saul, still breathing threats and murder against the disciples of the Lord, went to the high priest, and asked for letters from him to the synagogues at Damascus, so that if he found any belonging to the Way, both men and women, he might bring them bound to Jerusalem. And it came about that as he journeyed, he was approaching Damascus, and suddenly a light from heaven flashed around him; and he fell to the ground, and heard a voice saying to him, 'Saul, Saul, why are you persecuting Me?' And he said, 'Who art Thou, Lord?' And He said, 'I am Jesus whom you are persecuting, but rise, and enter the city, and it shall be told you what you must do.' And the men who traveled with him stood speechless, hearing the voice, but seeing no one. And Saul got up from the ground, and though his eyes were open, he could see nothing; and leading him by the hand, they brought him into Damascus. And he was three days without sight, and neither ate nor drank.

"Now there was a certain disciple at Damascus, named Ananias; and the Lord said to him in a vision, 'Ananias.' And he said, 'Behold, here am I, Lord.' And the Lord said to him 'Arise and go to the street called Straight, and inquire at the house of Judas for a man from Tarsus named Saul, for behold, he is praying, and he has seen in a vision a man named Ananias come in and lay his hands on him, so that he might regain his sight'" (Acts 9:1–12).

At this point one can see why Christians feared Paul. Ananias answered: "'Lord, I have heard from many about this man, how much harm he did to Thy saints at Jerusalem; and here he has authority from the chief priests to bind all who call upon Thy name.' But the Lord said to him, 'Go, for he is a chosen instrument of Mine, to bear My name before the Gentiles and kings and the sons of Israel; for I will show him how much he must suffer for My name's sake.' And Ananias departed and entered the house, and after laying his hands on him said, 'Brother Saul, the Lord Jesus, who appeared to you on the road by which you were coming, has sent me so that you may regain your sight, and be filled with the Holy Spirit.' And immediately there fell from his eyes something like scales, and he regained his sight, and he arose and was baptized; and he took food and was strengthened" (Acts 9:13–19a). Paul said, "Have I not seen Jesus our Lord?" (1 Corinthians 9:1). He compared Christ's appearance to him with Christ's postresurrection appearances among the apostles. "And last of all . . . He appeared to me also" (1 Corinthians 15:8).

Not only did Paul see Jesus, but he saw him in an irresistible way. He didn't proclaim the gospel out of choice but from necessity. "For if I preach the gospel, I have nothing to boast of, for I am under compulsion" (1 Corinthians 9:16).

Notice that Paul's encounter with Jesus and subsequent conversion were sudden and unexpected. "A very bright light suddenly flashed from heaven all around me" (Acts 22:6). Paul had no idea who this heavenly person could be. The announcement that it was Jesus of Nazareth left him trembling and astonished.

We might not know all the details, chronology, or psychology of what happened to Paul on the road to Damascus but we do know this: it radically affected every area of his life.

First, Paul's character was drastically transformed. *The Encyclopaedia Britannica* describes him before his conversion as an intolerant, bitter, persecuting, religious bigot—proud and temperamental. After his conversion he is pictured as patient, kind, enduring, and self-sacrificing.[1c] Kenneth Scott Latourette says: "What integrated Paul's life, however, and lifted this almost neurotic temperament out of obscurity into enduring influence was a profound and revolutionary religious experience."[3]

Second, Paul's relationship with the followers of Jesus was transformed. "Now for several days he was with the disciples who were at Damascus" (Acts 9:19). And when Paul went to the apostles, he received the "right hand of fellowship."

Third, Paul's message was transformed. Though he still loved his Jewish heritage, he had changed

from a bitter antagonist to a determined protago-
nist of the Christian faith. "Immediately he began
to proclaim Jesus in the synagogues, saying, 'He is
the Son of God'" (Acts 9:20). Paul's intellectual
convictions had changed. His experience compelled him to acknowledge that Jesus was the
Messiah, in direct conflict with the Pharisees'
messianic ideas. His new conception of Christ
meant a total revolution in his thought.[4] Jacques
Dupont acutely observes that after Paul "had
passionately denied that a crucified man could be
the Messiah, he came to grant that Jesus was
indeed the Messiah, and, as a consequence, re-
thought all his messianic ideas."[2]

Also he could now understand that Christ's
death on the cross, which appeared to be a curse
of God and a deplorable ending of someone's life,
was actually God through Christ reconciling the
world to himself. Paul came to understand that
through the crucifixion Christ became a curse for
us (Galatians 3:13) and was "made . . . to be sin
on our behalf" (2 Corinthians 5:21). Instead of a
defeat, the death of Christ was a great victory,
being capped by the resurrection. The cross was
no longer a "stumbling block" but the essence of
God's messianic redemption. Paul's missionary
preaching can be summarized as "explaining and
giving evidence that the Christ had to suffer and
rise again from the dead . . . 'This Jesus whom I
am proclaiming to you is the Christ,'" he said
(Acts 17:3).

Did You Hear What Happened to Saul?

Fourth, Paul's mission was transformed. He was changed from a Gentile-hater to a missionary to Gentiles. He was changed from a Jewish zealot to an evangelist to Gentiles. As a Jew and Pharisee, Paul looked down upon the despised Gentile as someone inferior to God's chosen people. The Damascus experience changed him into a dedicated apostle, with his life's mission aimed toward helping the Gentile. Paul saw in the Christ who appeared to him the Savior for all people. Paul went from being an orthodox Pharisee whose mission was to preserve strict Judaism to being a propagator of that new radical sect called Christianity which he had so violently opposed. There was such a change in him that "all those hearing him continued to be amazed, and were saying 'Is this not he who in Jerusalem destroyed those who called on this [Jesus'] name, and who had come here for the purpose of bringing them bound before the chief priests?'" (Acts 9:21).

Historian Philip Schaff states: "The conversion of Paul marks not only a turning-point in his personal history, but also an important epoch in the history of the apostolic church, and consequently in the history of mankind. It was the most fruitful event since the miracle of Pentecost, and secured the universal victory of Christianity."[5]

During lunch at the University of Houston, I sat down next to a student. As we discussed Christianity he made the statement that there wasn't any historical evidence for Christianity or Christ.

He was a history major and I noticed that one of his books was a Roman history textbook. He acknowledged that there was a chapter dealing with the Apostle Paul and Christianity. After reading the chapter, the student found it interesting that the section on Paul started by describing the life of Saul of Tarsus and ended with a description of the life of the Apostle Paul. In the next to the last paragraph the book observed that what happened in between was not clear. After I turned to the book of Acts and explained Christ's postresurrection appearance to Paul, this student saw that it was the most logical explanation of Paul's conversion. Later he also trusted Christ as his Savior.

Elias Andrews comments: "Many have found in the radical transformation of this 'Pharisee of the Pharisees' the most convincing evidence of the truth and the power of the religion to which he was converted, as well as the ultimate worth and place of the Person of Christ."[1d] Archibald Mac-Bride, professor at the University of Aberdeen, writes of Paul: "Beside his achievements . . . the achievements of Alexander and Napoleon pale into insignificance."[6] Clement says that Paul "bore chains seven times; preached the gospel in the East and West; came to the limit of the West; and died a martyr under the rulers."[7]

Paul stated again and again that the living, resurrected Jesus had transformed his life. He was so convinced of Christ's resurrection from the dead that he, too, died a martyr's death for his beliefs.

Two professors at Oxford, Gilbert West and Lord Lyttleton, were determined to destroy the basis of the Christian faith. West was going to demonstrate the fallacy of the resurrection and Lyttleton was going to prove that Saul of Tarsus had never converted to Christianity. Both men came to the opposite conclusion and became ardent followers of Jesus. Lord Lyttleton writes: "The conversion and apostleship of Saint Paul alone, duly considered, was of itself a demonstration sufficient to prove Christianity to be a Divine Revelation."[8] He concludes that if Paul's twenty-five years of suffering and service for Christ were a reality, then his conversion was true, for everything he did began with that sudden change. And if his conversion was true, Jesus Christ rose from the dead, for everything Paul was and did he attributed to the sight of the risen Christ.

NOTES ON CHAPTER 7

1. *The Encyclopaedia Britannica*, William Benton, Publisher. (Chicago: Encyclopaedia Britannica, Inc., 1970), Vol. 17, (a) p. 469; (b) p. 476; (c) p. 473; (d) p. 469.
2. Jacques Dupont, "The Conversion of Paul, and Its Influence on His Understanding of Salvation by Faith," *Apostolic History and the Gospel*. Edited by W. Ward Gasque and Ralph P. Martin (Grand Rapids: Wm. B. Eerdmans Publishing Co., 1970), p. 177; p. 76.

3. Kenneth Scott Latourette, *A History of Christianity* (New York: Harper & Row, 1953), p. 76.
4. W. J. Sparrow-Simpson, *The Resurrection and the Christian Faith* (Grand Rapids: Zondervan Publishing House, 1968), pp. 185–186.
5. Philip Schaff, *History of the Christian Church*, Vol. I. Apostolic Christianity, A.D. 1–100 (Grand Rapids: Wm. B. Eerdmans Publishing Co., 1910), p. 296.
6. *Chambers's Encyclopedia* (London: Pergamon Press, 1966), Vol. 10, p. 516.
7. Philip Schaff, *History of the Apostolic Church* (New York: Charles Scribner, 1857), p. 340.
8. George Lyttleton, *The Conversion of St. Paul* (New York: American Tract Society, 1929), p. 467.

8

Can You Keep a Good Man Down?

A student at the University of Uruguay said to me, "Professor McDowell, why can't you refute Christianity?" I answered, "For a very simple reason. I'm unable to explain away an event in history—the resurrection of Jesus Christ."

After more than 700 hours of studying this subject and thoroughly investigating its foundation, I came to the conclusion that the resurrection of Jesus Christ is either one of the most wicked, vicious, heartless hoaxes ever foisted upon people, or it is the most important fact of history.

The resurrection issue takes the question "Is Christianity valid?" out of the realm of philosophy and makes it a question of history. Does Christianity have a historically acceptable basis?

Is sufficient evidence available to warrant belief in the resurrection?

Some facts relevant to the resurrection are these: Jesus of Nazareth, a Jewish prophet who claimed to be the Christ prophesied in the Jewish Scriptures, was arrested, judged a political criminal, and crucified. Three days after his death and burial, some women who went to his tomb found the body gone. His disciples claimed that God had raised him from the dead and that he had appeared to them various times before ascending into heaven.

From this foundation, Christianity spread throughout the Roman Empire and has continued to exert great influence down through the centuries.

Did the resurrection actually happen?

JESUS' BURIAL

The body of Jesus, in accordance with Jewish burial customs, was wrapped in a linen cloth. About 100 pounds of aromatic spices, mixed together to form a gummy substance, were applied to the wrappings of cloth about the body.[1]

After the body was placed in a solid rock tomb,[2] an extremely large stone (weighing approximately two tons) was rolled by means of levers against the entrance of the tomb.[3]

A Roman guard of strictly disciplined men was

stationed to guard the tomb. Fear of punishment "produced flawless attention to duty, especially in the night watches."[4] This guard affixed on the tomb the Roman seal, a stamp of Roman power and authority.[5] The seal was meant to prevent vandalizing. Anyone trying to move the stone from the tomb's entrance would have broken the seal and thus incurred the wrath of Roman law.

But the tomb was empty.

THE EMPTY TOMB

The followers of Jesus said he had risen from the dead. They reported that he appeared to them during a period of forty days, showing himself to them by many "convincing proofs" (some versions say "infallible proofs").[6] Paul the apostle said that Jesus appeared to more than 500 of his followers at one time, the majority of whom were still alive and could confirm what Paul wrote.[7]

A. M. Ramsey writes: "I believe in the Resurrection, partly because a series of facts are unaccountable without it."[8] The empty tomb was "too notorious to be denied." Paul Althaus states that the resurrection "could not have been maintained in Jerusalem for a single day, for a single hour, if the emptiness of the tomb had not been established as a fact for all concerned."[9]

Paul L. Maier concludes: "If all the evidence is weighed carefully and fairly, it is indeed justifiable, according to the canons of historical research, to conclude that the tomb in which Jesus was buried was actually empty on the morning of the first Easter. And no shred of evidence has yet been discovered in literary sources, epigraphy, or archaeology that would disprove this statement."[10]

How can we explain the empty tomb? Can it possibly be accounted for by a natural cause?

Based on overwhelming historical evidence, Christians believe that Jesus was bodily resurrected in time and space by the supernatural power of God. The difficulties of belief may be great, but the problems inherent in unbelief present even greater difficulties.

The situation at the tomb after the resurrection is significant. The Roman seal was broken, which meant automatic crucifixion upside down for those who did it. The large stone was moved up and away from not just the entrance, but from the entire massive sepulchre, looking as if it had been picked up and carried away.[11] The guard unit had fled. Justin in his *Digest* 49.16 lists eighteen offenses for which a guard unit could be put to death. These included falling asleep or leaving one's position unguarded.

The women came and found the tomb empty; they panicked, and went back and told the men. Peter and John ran to the tomb. John got there first but he didn't enter it. He looked in and there were the grave clothes, caved in a little, but empty. The body of Christ had passed right through them into a new existence. Let's face it, that would make you quite a believer, at least for the moment.

The theories advanced to explain the resurrection from natural causes are weak; they actually help to build confidence in the truth of the resurrection.

THE WRONG TOMB?

A theory propounded by Kirsopp Lake assumes that the women who reported the body missing had mistakenly gone to the wrong tomb. If so, then the disciples who went to check up on the women's statement must also have gone to the wrong tomb. We can be certain, however, that the Jewish authorities, who had asked for that Roman guard to be stationed at the tomb to prevent the body from being stolen, wouldn't have been mistaken about the location. Nor would the Roman guards, for they were there.

If a wrong tomb were involved, the Jewish authorities would have lost no time in producing the body from the proper tomb, thus effectively quenching for all time any rumor of a resurrection.

Another attempt at explanation claims that the appearances of Jesus after the resurrection were either illusions or hallucinations. Unsupported by the psychological principles governing the appearances of hallucinations, this theory also does not coincide with the historical situation or with the mental state of the apostles.

So, where was the actual body, and why wasn't it produced?

SWOON THEORY

Popularized by Venturini several centuries ago and often quoted today, the swoon theory says that Jesus didn't really die; he merely fainted from exhaustion and loss of blood. Everyone thought him dead, but later he was resuscitated and the disciples thought it to be a resurrection.

The skeptic David Friedrich Strauss—himself no believer in the resurrection—gave the death-blow to any thought that Jesus revived from a swoon: "It is impossible that a being who had stolen half-dead out of the sepulchre, who crept about weak and ill, wanting medical treatment, who required bandaging, strengthening and in-dulgence, and who still at last yielded to his sufferings, could have given to the disciples the impression that he was a Conqueror over death and the grave, the Prince of Life, an impression which lay at the bottom of their future ministry. Such a resuscitation could only have weakened the impression which He had made upon them in life and in death, at the most could only have given it an elegiac voice, but could by no possibil-ity have changed their sorrow into enthusiasm, have elevated their reverence into worship."[12]

THE BODY STOLEN?

Another theory maintains that the body was stolen by the disciples while the guard slept.[13] The depression and cowardice of the disciples provide a hardhitting argument against their suddenly becoming so brave and daring as to face a detachment of soldiers at the tomb and steal the body. They were in no mood to attempt anything like that.

J. N. D. Anderson has been dean of the faculty of law at the University of London, chairman of the department of Oriental law at the School of Oriental and African Studies, and director of the Institute of Advanced Legal Studies at the University of London. Commenting on the proposition that the disciples stole Christ's body, he says: "This would run totally contrary to all we know of them: their ethical teaching, the quality of their lives, their steadfastness in suffering and persecution. Nor would it begin to explain their dramatic transformation from dejected and dispirited escapists into witnesses whom no opposition could muzzle."[14]

The theory that the Jewish or Roman authorities moved Christ's body is no more reasonable an explanation for the empty tomb than theft by the disciples. If the authorities had the body in their possession or knew where it was, why, when the disciples were preaching the resurrection in Jerusalem, didn't they explain that they had taken it?

If they had, why didn't they explain exactly

where the body lay? Why didn't they recover the corpse, put it on a cart, and wheel it through the center of Jerusalem? Such an action would certainly have destroyed Christianity.

Dr. John Warwick Montgomery comments: "It passes the bounds of credibility that the early Christians could have manufactured such a tale and then preached it among those who might easily have refuted it simply by producing the body of Jesus."[15]

EVIDENCE FOR THE RESURRECTION

Professor Thomas Arnold, for fourteen years the headmaster of Rugby, author of a famous three-volume *History of Rome*, and appointed to the chair of modern history at Oxford, was well acquainted with the value of evidence in determining historical facts. He said: "I have been used for many years to study the histories of other times, and to examine and weigh the evidence of those who have written about them, and I know of no one fact in the history of mankind which is proved by better and fuller evidence of every sort, to the understanding of a fair inquirer, than the great sign which God has given us that Christ died and rose again from the dead."[16]

English scholar Brooke Foss Westcott said: "Taking all the evidence together, it is not too much to say that there is no historic incident better or more variously supported than the resurrection of Christ. Nothing but the antecedent assumption that it must be false could have suggested the idea of deficiency in the proof of it."[17]

Dr. Simon Greenleaf was one of the greatest legal minds we have had in this country. He was the famous Royall Professor of Law at Harvard University, and succeeded Justice Joseph Story as the Dane Professor of Law in the same university. H. W. H. Knotts in the *Dictionary of American Biography* says of him: "To the efforts of Story and Greenleaf is ascribed the rise of the Harvard Law School to its eminent position among the legal schools of the United States." While professor of law at Harvard, Greenleaf wrote a volume in which he examined the legal value of the apostles' testimony to the resurrection of Christ. He observed that it was impossible that the apostles "could have persisted in affirming the truths they had narrated, had not Jesus actually risen from the dead, and had they not known this fact as certainly as they knew any other fact."[18] Greenleaf concluded that the resurrection of Christ was one of the best supported events in history, according to the laws of legal evidence administered in courts of justice.

Another lawyer, Frank Morison, set out to refute the evidence for the resurrection. He thought that the life of Jesus was one of the most beautiful lives ever lived, but when it came to the resurrection he thought someone had come along and tacked a myth onto the story of Jesus. He planned to write an account of the last few days of Jesus. He would of course disregard the resurrection. He figured that an intelligent, rational approach to Jesus would completely discount his resurrection. However, upon approaching the facts with his legal background and training, he had to change his mind. He eventually wrote a best-seller, *Who Moved the Stone?* The first chapter was titled, "The Book That Refused to Be Written," and the rest of the chapters deal decisively with the evidence for Christ's resurrection.[19]

George Eldon Ladd concludes: "The only rational explanation for these historical facts is that God raised Jesus in bodily form."[20] A believer in Jesus Christ today can have complete confidence, as did the first Christians, that his faith is based, not on myth or legend, but on the solid historical fact of the risen Christ and the empty tomb.

Most important of all, the individual believer can experience the power of the risen Christ in his life today. First of all, he can know that his sins are forgiven.[21] Second, he can be assured of eternal life and his own resurrection from the grave.[22] Third, he can be released from a meaningless and empty life and be transformed into a new creature in Jesus Christ.[23]

What is your evaluation and decision? What do you think of the empty tomb? After examining the evidence from a judicial perspective, Lord Darling, former Chief Justice of England, concluded that "there exists such overwhelming evidence, positive and negative, factual and circumstantial, that no intelligent jury in the world could fail to bring in a verdict that the resurrection story is true."[24]

NOTES ON CHAPTER 8

1. John 19:39, 40.
2. Matthew 27:60.
3. Mark 16:4.
4. George Currie, *The Military Discipline of the Romans from the Founding of the City to the Close of the Republic.* An abstract of a thesis published under the auspices of the Graduate Council of Indiana University, 1928, pp. 41–43.
5. A. T. Robertson, *Word Pictures in the New Testament* (New York: R. R. Smith, Inc., 1931), p. 239.
6. Acts 1:3.
7. 1 Corinthians 15:3–8.
8. Arthur Michael Ramsey, *God, Christ and the World* (London: SCM Press, 1969), pp. 78–80.
9. Paul Althaus, *Die Wahrheit des kirchlichen Osterglaubens* (Gütersloh: C. Bertelsmann, 1941), pp. 22, 25ff.
10. *Independent, Press-Telegram*, Long Beach, Calif., Saturday, April 21, 1973, p. A-10.
11. Josh McDowell, *Evidence That Demands a Verdict* (San Bernardino, Calif: Campus Crusade for Christ International, 1973), p. 231.
12. David Frederick Strauss, *The Life of Jesus for the People* (London: Williams and Norgate, 1879, 2nd ed.), Vol. 1, p. 412.
13. Matthew 28:1–15.
14. J. N. D. Anderson, *Christianity: The Witness of History*, copyright Tyndale Press, 1970. Used by permission of InterVarsity Press, Downers Grove, Ill., p. 92.

15. John Warwick Montgomery, *History and Christianity* (Downers Grove, Ill.: InterVarsity Press, 1972), p. 78.

16. Thomas Arnold, *Christian Life—Its Hopes, Its Fears, and Its Close* (London: T. Fellowes, 1859, 6th ed.), p. 324.

17. Paul E. Little, *Know Why You Believe* (Wheaton: Scripture Press Publications, Inc., 1967), p. 70.

18. Simon Greenleaf, *An Examination of the Testimony of the Four Evangelists by the Rules of Evidence Administered in the Courts of Justice* (Grand Rapids: Baker Book House, 1965. Reprint of 1874 edition. New York: J. Cockroft and Co., 1874), p. 29.

19. Frank Morison, *Who Moved the Stone?* (London: Faber and Faber, 1930).

20. George Eldon Ladd, *I Believe in the Resurrection of Jesus* (Grand Rapids: William B. Eerdmans Publishing Co., 1975), p. 141.

21. 1 Corinthians 15:3.

22. 1 Corinthians 15:19–26.

23. John 10:10; 2 Corinthians 5:17.

24. Michael Green, *Man Alive* (Downers Grove, Ill.: Inter-Varsity Press, 1968), p. 54.

9

Will the Real Messiah Please Stand Up?

Jesus had various credentials to support his claims to being the Messiah, God's Son. In this chapter I want to deal with one credential often overlooked, one of the most profound: the fulfillment of prophecy in his life.

Over and over again Jesus appealed to the prophecies of the Old Testament to substantiate his claims as the Messiah. Galatians 4:4 says, "But when the fulness of the time came, God sent forth His Son, born of a woman, born under the Law." Here we have reference to the prophecies being fulfilled in Jesus Christ. "And beginning with Moses and with all the prophets he explained to them the things concerning Himself in all the Scriptures" (Luke 24:27). Jesus said to them, "These are My words which I spoke to you while I was still with you, that all things which are written about Me in the Law of Moses and the Prophets and the Psalms must be fulfilled" (v. 44). He said, "For if you believed Moses, you would believe Me; for he wrote of Me" (John 5:46). He said, "Abraham rejoiced to see My day" (John 8:56). The apostles, the New Testament writers, etc., constantly appealed to fulfilled prophecy to substantiate the claims of Jesus as the Son of God, the Savior, the Messiah. "But the things which God announced beforehand by the mouth of all the prophets, that His Christ should suffer, He has thus fulfilled" (Acts 3:18). "And according to Paul's custom, he went to them, and for three Sabbaths reasoned with them from the Scriptures [meaning the Old Testament], explaining and giving evidence that the Christ had to suffer and rise again from the dead, and saying, 'This Jesus whom I am proclaiming to you is the Christ'" (Acts 17:2, 3). "For I delivered to you as of first importance what I also received, that Christ died for our sins according to the Scriptures [in other words, Christ's death was prophesied in the Old Testament], and that He was buried, and that He was raised on the third day according to the Scriptures" (1 Corinthians 15:3, 4).

In the Old Testament there are sixty major messianic prophecies and approximately 270 ramifications that were fulfilled in one person, Jesus Christ. It is helpful to look at all these predictions fulfilled in Christ as his "address."

You've probably never realized how important the details of *your* name and address are—and yet these details set you apart from the four billion other people who also inhabit this planet.

AN ADDRESS IN HISTORY

With even greater detail, God wrote an "address" in history to single out his Son, the Messiah, the Savior of mankind, from anyone who has ever lived in history—past, present, and future. The specifics of this "address" can be found in the Old Testament, a document written over a period of 1,000 years which contains over 300 references to his coming. Using the science of probability, we find the chances of just forty-eight of these prophecies being fulfilled in one person to be only one in ten[157].

The task of matching up God's address with one man is further complicated by the fact that all the prophecies of the Messiah were made at least 400 years before he was to appear. Some might disagree and say that these prophecies were written down after the time of Christ and fabricated to coincide with his life. This might sound feasible until you realize that the Septuagint, the Greek translation of the Hebrew Old Testament, was translated around 150–200 B.C. This Greek translation shows that there was at least a two-hundred-year gap between the prophecies being recorded and their fulfillment in Christ.

Certainly God was writing an "address" in history that only the Messiah could fulfill. There have been approximately forty major claims by men to be the Jewish Messiah. But only one—Jesus Christ—appealed to fulfilled prophecy to substantiate his claims, and only his credentials back up those claims.

What were some of those details? And what events had to precede and coincide with the appearance of God's Son?

To begin, we need to go way back to Genesis 3:15. Here we have the first messianic prophecy. In all of Scripture, only one Man was "born of the seed of a woman"—all others are born of the seed of a man. Here is one who will come into the world and undo the works of Satan ("bruise his head").

In Genesis 9 and 10 God narrowed the "address" down further. Noah had three sons, Shem, Japheth, and Ham. Today all of the nations of the world can be traced back to these three men. But in this statement, God effectively eliminated two-thirds of them from the line of Messiahship. The Messiah will come through the lineage of Shem.

Then, continuing on down to the year 2000 B.C., we find God calling a man named Abraham out of Ur of the Chaldees. With Abraham, God became still more specific, stating that the Messiah will be one of his descendants.[1] All the families of the earth will be blessed through Abraham. When

Abraham had two sons, Isaac and Ishmael, many of Abraham's descendants were eliminated when God selected his second son, Isaac.[2]

Isaac had two sons, Jacob and Esau, and then God chose the line of Jacob.[3] Jacob had twelve sons, out of whom developed the twelve tribes of Israel. Then God singled out the tribe of Judah for Messiahship and eliminated $^{11}/_{12}$ths of the Israelite tribes. And of all the family lines within Judah's tribe, the line of Jesse was the divine choice.[4] One can see the probability building.

Jesse had eight children and in 2 Samuel 7:12–16 and Jeremiah 23:5 God eliminated $^{7}/_{8}$ths of Jesse's family line: we read that God's Man will not only be of the seed of a woman, the lineage of Shem, the race of the Jews, the line of Isaac, the line of Jacob, the tribe of Judah, but that he will also be of the house of David.

A prophecy dating 1012 B.C.[5] also predicts that this Man's hands and feet will be pierced (i.e., he will be crucified). This description was written 800 years before crucifixion was put into effect by the Romans.

Isaiah 7:14 adds that he will be born of a virgin: a natural birth of unnatural conception, a criterion beyond human planning and control. Several prophecies recorded in Isaiah and the Psalms[6] describe the social climate and response that God's man will encounter: his own people, the Jews, will reject him and the Gentiles will believe in him. There will be a forerunner for him (Isaiah

105

40:3; Malachi 3:1), a voice in the wilderness, one preparing the way before the Lord, a John the Baptist.

THIRTY PIECES OF SILVER

Notice, too, the seven ramifications of a prophecy[7] that narrows the drama down even further. Here God indicates that the Messiah will (1) be betrayed, (2) by a friend, (3) for thirty pieces, (4) of silver, and that it will be (5) cast on the floor, (6) of the temple, and (7) used to buy a potter's field.

In Micah 5:2 God eliminated all the cities of the world and selected Bethlehem, with less than 1,000 people, as the Messiah's birthplace.

Then through a series of prophecies he even defined the time sequence that would set his Man apart. For example, Malachi 3:1 and four other Old Testament verses[8] require the Messiah to come while the temple of Jerusalem is still standing. This is of great significance when we realize that the temple was destroyed in A.D. 70 and has not since been rebuilt.

The precise lineage; the place, time, and manner of birth; people's reactions, the betrayal; the manner of death. These are just a fragment of the hundreds of details that made up the "address" to identify God's Son, the Messiah, the Savior of the world.

OBJECTION: SUCH FULFILLED PROPHECY WAS COINCIDENTAL

"Why, you could find some of these prophecies fulfilled in Kennedy, King, Nasser, etc.," replies a critic.

Yes, one could possibly find one or two prophecies fulfilled in other men, but not all sixty major prophecies and 270 ramifications. In fact, if you can find someone, other than Jesus, either living or dead, who can fulfill only half of the predictions concerning Messiah which are given in *Messiah in Both Testaments* by Fred John Meldau, the Christian Victory Publishing Company of Denver is ready to give you a $1,000 reward.

H. Harold Hartzler, of the American Scientific Affiliation, in the foreword of a book by Peter W. Stoner writes: "The manuscript for *Science Speaks* has been carefully reviewed by a committee of the American Scientific Affiliation members and by the Executive Council of the same group and has been found, in general, to be dependable and accurate in regard to the scientific material presented. The mathematical analysis included is based upon principles of probability which are thoroughly sound, and Professor Stoner has applied these principles in a proper and convincing way."[9]

The following probabilities are taken from that book to show that coincidence is ruled out by the science of probability. Stoner says that by using the modern science of probability in reference to eight prophecies, "we find that the chance that any man might have lived down to the present time and fulfilled all eight prophecies is 1 in 10^{17}." That would be 1 in 100,000,000,000,000,000. In order to help us comprehend this staggering probability, Stoner illustrates it by supposing that "we take 10^{17} silver dollars and lay them on the face of Texas. They will cover all of the state two feet deep. Now mark one of these silver dollars and stir the whole mass thoroughly, all over the state. Blindfold a man and tell him that he can travel as far as he wishes, but he must pick up one silver dollar and say that this is the right one. What chance would he have of getting the right one? Just the same chance that the prophets would have had of writing these eight prophecies and having them all come true in any one man, from their day to the present time, providing they wrote them in their own wisdom.

"Now these prophecies were either given by inspiration of God or the prophets just wrote them as they thought they should be. In such a case the prophets had just one chance in 10^{17} of having them come true in any man, but they all came true in Christ.

"This means that the fulfillment of these eight prophecies alone proves that God inspired the writing of those prophecies to a definiteness which lacks only one chance in 10^{17} of being absolute."[9]

ANOTHER OBJECTION

Another objection is that Jesus deliberately attempted to fulfill the Jewish prophecies. This objection seems plausible until we realize that many of the details of the Messiah's coming were totally beyond human control. For example, the place of birth. I can just hear Jesus in Mary's womb as she rode on the donkey: "Mom, we won't make it . . ." When Herod asked the chief priests and scribes, "Where is the Christ to be born?" they said, "In Bethlehem of Judea, for so it has been written by the prophet" (Matthew 2:5). The time of his coming. The manner of his birth. Betrayal by Judas and the betrayal price. The manner of his death. The people's reaction, the mocking and spitting, the staring. The casting of dice for his clothes. The non-tearing of his garment, etc. Half the prophecies are beyond his fulfillment. He couldn't work it out to be born of the seed of the woman, the lineage of Shem, the descendants of Abraham, etc. No wonder Jesus and the apostles appealed to fulfilled prophecy to substantiate his claim.

Why did God go to all this trouble? I believe he wanted Jesus Christ to have all the credentials he needed when he came into the world. Yet the most exciting thing about Jesus Christ is that he came to change lives. He alone proved correct the hundreds of Old Testament prophecies that described his coming. And he alone can fulfill the greatest prophecy of all for those who will accept

109

it—the promise of new life: "I will give you a new heart and put a new spirit within you. . . . Therefore if any man is in Christ, he is a new creature; the old things passed away; behold, new things have come."[10]

NOTES ON CHAPTER 9

1. Genesis 12; 17; 22.
2. Genesis 17; 21.
3. Genesis 28; 35:10–12; Numbers 24:17.
4. Isaiah 11:1–5.
5. Psalm 22:6–18; Zechariah 12:10; compare Galatians 3:13.
6. Isaiah 8:14; 28:16; 49:6; 50:6; 52:53; 60:3; Psalm 22:7, 8; 118:22.
7. Zechariah 11:11–13; Psalm 41; compare Jeremiah 32:6–15 and Matthew 27:3–10.
8. Psalm 118:26; Daniel 9:26; Zechariah 11:13; Haggai 2:7–9. For a more complete discussion of the Daniel 9 prophecy, see pp. 178–181 of my book *Evidence That Demands a Verdict*.
9. Peter W. Stoner, and Robert C. Newman, *Science Speaks* (Chicago: Moody Press, 1976), pp. 106–112.
10. Ezekiel 36:25–27; 2 Corinthians 5:17.

10
Isn't There Some Other Way?

Recently at the University of Texas a graduate student approached me and asked, "Why is Jesus the only way to a relationship with God?" I had shown that Jesus claimed to be the only way to God, that the testimony of the Scriptures and the apostles was reliable, and that there was sufficient evidence to warrant faith in Jesus as Savior and Lord. Yet he had the question, "Why Jesus? Isn't there some other way to a relationship with God? What about Buddha? Mohammed? Can't an individual simply live a good life? If God is such a loving God, then wouldn't he accept all people just the way they are?"

A businessman said to me, "Evidently you have proven that Jesus Christ is the Son of God. Aren't there other ways also to a relationship with God apart from Jesus?"

The above comments are indicative of many people's questions today about why one has to trust Jesus as Savior and Lord in order to have a relationship with God and experience the forgiveness of sin. I answered the student by saying that many people don't understand the nature of God. Usually the question is "How can a loving God allow a sinful individual to go to hell?" I would ask, "How can a holy, just, righteous God allow a sinful individual into his presence?" A misunderstanding of the basic nature and character of God has been the cause of so many theological and ethical problems. Most people understand God to be a loving God and they don't go any further. The problem is that God is not only a God of love. He is also a righteous, just, and holy God.

We basically know God through his attributes. An attribute is not a part of God. I used to think that if I took all the attributes of God—holiness, love, justice, righteousness—and added them up, the sum total would equal God. Well, that's not true. An attribute isn't something that is a part of God but something that is true of God. For example, when we say God is love, we don't mean that a part of God is love, but that love is something that is true of God. When God loves he is simply being himself.

Here is a problem that developed as a result of humanity entering into sin. God in eternity past decided to create man and woman. Basically I believe that the Bible indicates he created man and woman in order to share his love and glory with them. But when Adam and Eve rebelled and went their own individual ways, sin entered the human race. At that point individuals became sinful or separated from God. This is the "predicament" that God found himself in. He created men and women to share his glory with them, yet they spurned his counsel and command and chose to sin. And so he approached them with his love to save them. But because he is not only a loving God, but a holy, just, righteous God, his very nature would destroy any sinful individual. The Bible says, "For the wages of sin is death." So, you might say, God had a problem.

Within the Godhead—God the Father, God the Son, and God the Holy Spirit—a decision was made. Jesus, God the Son, would take upon himself human flesh. He would become the God-man. This is described in John 1 where it says that the Word became flesh and tabernacled or dwelt among us. And also in Philippians 2 where it says that Christ Jesus emptied himself and took on the form of a man.

Jesus was the God-man. He was just as much man as if he had never been God and just as much God as if he had never been man. By his own choice he lived a sinless life, wholly obeying the Father. The biblical declaration that "the wages of sin is death" did not apply to him. Because he was

113

not only finite man but infinite God, he had the infinite capacity to take upon himself the sins of the world. When he went to the cross almost 2000 years ago, a holy, just, righteous God poured out his wrath upon his Son. And when Jesus said, "It is finished," the just, righteous nature of God was satisfied. You could say that at that point God was "set free" to deal with humanity in love without having to destroy a sinful individual, because through Jesus' death on the cross, God's righteous nature was satisfied.

Often I ask people the question, "For whom did Jesus die?" and usually they reply, "For me" or "For the world." And I'll say, "Yes, that's right, but for whom else did Jesus die?" and usually they'll say, "Why, I don't know." I reply, "For God the Father." You see, Christ not only died for us but he also died for the Father. This is described in Romans 3 where it talks about propitiation. Propitiation basically means satisfaction of a requirement. And when Jesus died on the cross, he not only died for us but he died to meet the holy and just requirements of the basic nature of God.

An incident that took place several years ago in California illuminates what Jesus did on the cross in order to solve the problem God had in dealing with the sin of humanity. A young woman was picked up for speeding. She was ticketed and taken before the judge. The judge read off the citation and said, "Guilty or not guilty?" The woman replied, "Guilty." The judge brought down the gavel and fined her $100 or ten days. Then an amazing thing took place. The judge stood up, took off his robe, walked down around in front, took out his billfold, and paid the fine. What's the explanation of this? The judge was her father. He loved his daughter, yet he was a just judge. His daughter had broken the law and he couldn't simply say to her, "Because I love you so much, I forgive you. You may leave." If he had done that, he wouldn't have been a righteous judge. He wouldn't have upheld the law. But he loved his daughter so much that he was willing to take off his judicial robe and come down in front and represent her as her father and pay the fine.

This illustration pictures to some extent what God did for us through Jesus Christ. We sinned. The Bible says, "The wages of sin is death." No matter how much he loved us, God had to bring down the gavel and say *death*, because he is a righteous and just God. And yet, being a loving God, he loved us so much that he was willing to come down off the throne in the form of the man Christ Jesus and pay the price for us, which was Christ's death on the cross.

At this point many people ask the question, "Why couldn't God just forgive?" An executive of a large corporation said, "My employees often do something, break something, and I just forgive them." Then he added, "Are you trying to tell me I can do something that God can't do?" People fail to realize that wherever there is forgiveness there's a payment. For example, let's say my daughter breaks a lamp in my home. I'm a loving and forgiving father, so I put her on my lap, and I hug her and I say, "Don't cry, honey. Daddy loves you and forgives you." Now usually the person I tell that story to says, "Well, that's what God ought to do." Then I ask the question, "Who pays for the lamp?" The fact is, *I* do. There's always a price in forgiveness. Let's say somebody insults you in front of others and later you graciously say, "I forgive you." Who bears the price of the insult? You do.

This is what God has done. God has said, "I forgive you." But he was willing to pay the price himself through the cross.

11

He Changed My Life

Jesus Christ is alive. The fact that I'm alive and doing the things I do is evidence that Jesus Christ is raised from the dead.

Thomas Aquinas wrote: "There is within every soul a thirst for happiness and meaning." As a teen-ager I wanted to be happy. There's nothing wrong with that. I wanted to be one of the happiest individuals in the entire world. I also wanted meaning in life. I wanted answers to questions. "Who am I?" "Why in the world am I here?" "Where am I going?"

More than that, I wanted to be free. I wanted to be one of the freest individuals in the whole world. Freedom to me is not going out and doing what you want to do. Anyone can do that, and lots of people are doing it. Freedom is "to have the

117

power to do what you know you ought to do."
Most people know what they ought to do but they
don't have the power to do it. They're in bondage.

So I started looking for answers. It seems that
almost everyone is into some sort of religion, so I
did the obvious thing and took off for church. I
must have found the wrong church though. Some
of you know what I'm talking about: I felt worse
inside than I did outside. I went in the morning, I
went in the afternoon, and I went in the evening.

I'm always very practical, and when something
doesn't work, I chuck it. I chucked religion. The
only thing I ever got out of religion was the
twenty-five cents I put in the offering and the
thirty-five cents I took out for a milkshake. And
that's about all many people ever gain from "religion."

I began to wonder if prestige was the answer.
Being a leader, accepting some cause, giving yourself to it, and "being known" might do it. In the
first university I attended, the student leaders
held the purse strings and threw their weight
around. So I ran for freshman class president and
got elected. It was neat knowing everyone on
campus, having everyone say, "Hi, Josh," making
the decisions, spending the university's money,
the students' money, to get speakers I wanted. It
was great but it wore off like everything else I had
tried. I would wake up Monday morning, usually
with a headache because of the night before, and
my attitude was, "Well, here goes another five

days." I endured Monday through Friday. Happiness revolved around three nights a week: Friday, Saturday, and Sunday. Then the vicious cycle began all over again.

Oh, I fooled them in the university. They thought I was one of the happiest-go-lucky guys around. During the political campaigns we used the phrase, "Happiness is Josh." I threw more parties with student money than anyone else did, but they never realized my happiness was like so many other people's. It depended on my own circumstances. If things were going great for me, I was great. When things would go lousy, I was lousy.

I was like a boat out in the ocean being tossed back and forth by the waves, the circumstances. There is a biblical term to describe that type of living: hell. But I couldn't find anyone living any other way and I couldn't find anyone who could tell me how to live differently or give me the strength to do it. I had everyone telling me what I ought to do but none of them could give me the power to do it. I began to be frustrated.

I suspect that few people in the universities and colleges of this country were more sincere in trying to find meaning, truth, and purpose to life than I was. I hadn't found it yet, but I didn't realize that at first. In and around the university I noticed a small group of people: eight students and two faculty members, and there was something different about their lives. They seemed to

119

know why they believed what they believed. I like to be around people like that. I don't care if they don't agree with *me*. Some of my closest friends are opposed to some things I believe, but I admire a man or woman with conviction. (I don't meet many, but I admire them when I meet them.) That's why I sometimes feel more at home with some radical leaders than I do with many Christians. Some of the Christians I meet are so wishy-washy that I wonder if maybe 50 percent of them are masquerading as Christians. But the people in this small group seemed to know where they were going. That's unusual among university students.

The people I began to notice didn't just *talk* about love. They got involved. They seemed to be riding above the circumstances of university life. It appeared that everybody else was under a pile. One important thing I noticed was that they seemed to have a happiness, a state of mind not dependent on circumstances. They appeared to possess an inner, constant source of joy. They were disgustingly happy. They had something I didn't have.

Like the average student, when somebody had something I didn't have, I wanted it. That's why they have to lock up bicycles in colleges. If education were really the answer, the university would probably be the most morally upright society in existence. But it's not. So, I decided to make friends with these intriguing people.

Two weeks after that decision we were all

sitting around a table in the student union, six students and two faculty members. The conversation started to get around to God. If you're an insecure person and a conversation centers on God, you tend to put on a big front. Every campus or community has a big mouth, a guy who says, "Uh . . . Christianity, ha, ha. That's for the weaklings, it's not intellectual." (Usually, the bigger the mouth, the bigger the vacuum.)

They were bothering me, so finally I looked over at one of the students, a good-looking woman (I used to think all Christians were ugly); and I leaned back in my chair because I didn't want the others to think I was interested, and I said, "Tell me, what changed your lives? Why are your lives so different from the other students, the leaders on campus, the professors? Why?"

That young woman must have had a lot of conviction. She looked me straight in the eye, no smile, and said two words I never thought I'd hear as part of a solution in a university. She said, "Jesus Christ." I said, "Oh, for God's sake, don't give me that garbage. I'm fed up with religion; I'm fed up with the church; I'm fed up with the Bible. Don't give me that garbage about religion." She shot back, "Mister, I didn't say religion, I said Jesus Christ." She pointed out something I'd never known before. Christianity is not a religion. Religion is humans trying to work their way to God through good works. Christianity is God coming to men and women through Jesus Christ offering them a relationship with himself.

There are probably more people in universities with misconceptions about Christianity than anywhere else in the world. Recently I met a teaching assistant who remarked in a graduate seminar that "anyone who walks into a church becomes a Christian." I replied, "Does walking into a garage make you a car?" There is no correlation. A Christian is somebody who puts his trust in Christ.

My new friends challenged me intellectually to examine the claims that Jesus Christ is God's Son; that taking on human flesh, he lived among real men and woman and died on the cross for the sins of mankind, that he was buried and he arose three days later and could change a person's life in the twentieth century.

I thought this was a farce. In fact, I thought most Christians were walking idiots. I'd met some. I used to wait for a Christian to speak up in the classroom so I could tear him or her up one side and down the other, and beat the insecure professor to the punch. I imagined that if a Christian had a brain cell, it would die of loneliness. I didn't know any better.

But these people challenged me over and over. Finally, I accepted their challenge, but I did it out of pride, to refute them. But I didn't know there were facts. I didn't know there was evidence that a person could evaluate.

Finally, my mind came to the conclusion that

Jesus Christ must have been who he claimed to be. In fact, the background of my first two books was my setting out to refute Christianity. When I couldn't, I ended up becoming a Christian. I have now spent thirteen years documenting why I believe that faith in Jesus Christ is intellectually feasible.

At that time, though, I had quite a problem. My mind told me all this was true but my will was pulling me in another direction. I discovered that becoming a Christian was rather ego-shattering. Jesus Christ made a direct challenge to my will to trust him. Let me paraphrase him. "Look! I have been standing at the door and I am constantly knocking. If anyone hears me calling him and opens the door, I will come in" (Revelation 3:20). I didn't care if he did walk on water or turn water into wine. I didn't want any party pooper around. I couldn't think of a faster way to ruin a good time. So here was my mind telling me Christianity was true and my will was somewhere else.

Every time I was around those enthusiastic Christians, the conflict would begin. If you've ever been around happy people when you're miserable, you understand how they can bug you. They would be so happy and I would be so miserable that I'd literally get up and run right out of the student union. It came to the point where I'd go to bed at ten at night and I wouldn't get to sleep until four in the morning. I knew I had to get it off my mind before I went out of my mind! I was always open-minded, but not so open-minded that my brains would fall out.

But since I was open-minded, on December 19, 1959, at 8:30 P.M. during my second year at the university, I became a Christian.

Somebody asked me, "How do you know?" I said, "Look, I was there. It's changed my life." That night I prayed. I prayed four things to establish a relationship with the resurrected, living Christ which has since transformed my life.

First, I said, "Lord Jesus, thank you for dying on the cross for me." Second, I said, "I confess those things in my life that aren't pleasing to you and ask you to forgive me and cleanse me." (The Bible says, "Though your sins be as scarlet they shall be as white as snow.") Third, I said, "Right now, in the best way I know how, I open the door of my heart and life and trust you as my Savior and Lord. Take over the control of my life. Change me from the inside out. Make me the type of person you created me to be." The last thing I prayed was "Thank you for coming into my life by faith." It was a faith based not upon ignorance but upon evidence and the facts of history and God's Word.

I'm sure you've heard various religious people talking about their "bolt of lightning." Well, after I prayed, nothing happened. I mean nothing. And I still haven't sprouted wings. In fact, after I made that decision, I felt worse. I literally felt I was going to vomit. I felt sick deep down. "Oh no, what'd you get sucked into now?" I wondered. I really felt I'd gone off the deep end (and I'm sure some people think I did!).

I can tell you one thing: in six months to a year-and-a-half I found out that I hadn't gone off the deep end. My life *was* changed. I was in a debate with the head of the history department at a midwestern university and I said my life had been changed, and he interrupted me with "McDowell, are you trying to tell us that God really changed your life in the twentieth century? What areas?" After forty-five minutes he said, "Okay, that's enough."

One area I told him about was my restlessness. I always had to be occupied. I had to be over at my girl's place or somewhere else in a rap session. I'd walk across the campus and my mind was like a whirlwind with conflicts bouncing around the walls. I'd sit down and try to study or cogitate and I couldn't. But a few months after I made that decision for Christ, a kind of mental peace developed. Don't misunderstand. I'm not talking about the absence of conflict. What I found in this relationship with Jesus wasn't so much the absence of conflict but the ability to cope with it. I wouldn't trade that for anything in the world.

Another area that started to change was my bad temper. I used to blow my stack if somebody just looked at me cross-eyed. I still have the scars from almost killing a man my first year in the university. My temper was such a part of me that I didn't consciously seek to change it. I arrived at the crisis of losing my temper only to find it was gone! Only once in fourteen years have I lost my temper—and when I blew it that time, I made up for about six years!

There's another area of which I'm not proud. But I mention it because a lot of people need to have the same change in their lives, and I found the source of change: a relationship with the resurrected, living Christ. That area is hatred. I had a lot of hatred in my life. It wasn't something outwardly manifested, but there was a kind of inward grinding. I was ticked off with people, with things, with issues. Like so many other people, I was insecure. Every time I met someone different from me, he became a threat to me.

But I hated one man more than anyone else in the world. My father. I hated his guts. To me he was the town alcoholic. If you're from a small town and one of your parents is an alcoholic, you know what I'm talking about. Everybody knows. My friends would come to high school and make jokes about my father being downtown. They didn't think it bothered me. I was like other people, laughing on the outside, but let me tell you, I was crying on the inside. I'd go out in the barn and see my mother beaten so badly she couldn't get up, lying in the manure behind the cows. When we had friends over, I would take my father out, tie him up in the barn, and park the car up around the silo. We would tell our friends he'd had to go somewhere. I don't think anyone could have hated anyone more than I hated my father.

After I made that decision for Christ—maybe five months later—a love from God through Jesus Christ entered my life and was so strong it took that hatred and turned it upside down. I was able to look my father squarely in the eyes and say, "Dad, I love you." And I really meant it. After some of the things I'd done, that shook him up.

When I transferred to a private university I was in a serious car accident. My neck in traction, I was taken home. I'll never forget my father coming into my room. He asked me, "Son, how can you love a father like me?" I said, "Dad, six months ago I despised you." Then I shared with him my conclusions about Jesus Christ: "Dad, I let Christ come into my life. I can't explain it completely but as a result of that relationship I've found the capacity to love and accept not only you but other people just the way they are."

Forty-five minutes later one of the greatest thrills of my life occurred. Somebody in my own family, someone who knew me so well I couldn't pull the wool over his eyes, said to me, "Son, if God can do in my life what I've seen him do in yours, then I want to give him the opportunity." Right there my father prayed with me and trusted Christ.

Usually the changes take place over several days, weeks, or months, even a year. My life was changed in about six months to a year-and-a-half. The life of my father was changed right before my eyes. It was as if somebody reached down and turned on a light bulb. I've never seen such a rapid change before or since. My father touched whiskey only once after that. He got it as far as his lips and that was it. I've come to one conclusion. A relationship with Jesus Christ changes lives.

You can laugh at Christianity, you can mock and ridicule it. But it works. It changes lives. If you trust Christ, start watching your attitudes and actions, because Jesus Christ is in the business of changing lives.

But Christianity is not something you shove down somebody's throat or force on someone. You've got your life to live and I've got mine. All I can do is tell you what I've learned. After that, it's your decision.

Perhaps the prayer I prayed will help you: "Lord Jesus, I need you. Thank you for dying on the cross for me. Forgive me and cleanse me. Right this moment I trust you as Savior and Lord. Make me the type of person you created me to be. In Christ's name. Amen."